A California Childhood

A California Childhood

by
James Franco

INSIGHT
EDITIONS

San Rafael, California

For my Mom, dad, brothers, and Palo Alto friends.

So much of me is you.

♡

INSIGHT EDITIONS

PO Box 3088
San Rafael, CA 94912
www.insighteditions.com

"The Deer" was originally published in *Ploughshares*, spring 2012. "Camp" and
"Yosemite" reprinted with permission from Scribner, a Division of Simon &
Schuster, Inc., from PALO ALTO STORIES by James Franco. Copyright 2010
by WHOSE DOG R U Productions, Inc. All rights reserved.

Paintings on pages 36, 48, 49, and 107 were inspired by photos from the Palo Alto
High School Madrono Yearbook. Photos on pages 45, 82, 84, 95 (top), 96, 108, 116,
132, 144, and 153 are used with permission of the Palo Alto High School Madrono
Yearbook Program. Paintings on pages 46, 47, 50, 51, and 61 used with permission
of James Franco and Josh Smith. All other images used with permission and
courtesy of the Franco family.

Library of Congress Cataloging-in-Publication Data available.

ISBN: 978-1-60887-393-7

COLOPHON
Publisher—Raoul Goff
Art Director—Chrissy Kwasnik
Designer—Nicole Poor
Acquisitions Manager—Robbie Schmidt
Editor—Roxanna Aliaga
Associate Managing Editor—Jan Hughes
Production Manager—Jane Chinn
Additional editorial work by Elizabeth Mathews and Mikayla Butchart;
production support by Binh Matthews and Natalie Beaulieu.

Find us on Facebook: www.facebook.com/InsightEditions
Follow us on Twitter: @insighteditions

REPLANTED PAPER
Insight Editions, in association with Roots of Peace, will plant two trees for each tree used in the
manufacturing of this book. Roots of Peace is an internationally renowned humanitarian organization
dedicated to eradicating land mines worldwide and converting war-torn lands into productive farms
and wildlife habitats. Roots of Peace will plant two million fruit and nut trees in Afghanistan and
provide farmers there with the skills and support necessary for sustainable land use.

Manufactured in China by Insight Editions

10 9 8 7 6 5 4 3 2 1

Contents

me + mom
on the front porch

Introduction

If you are reading this, you have lived through a childhood. Post-1980 American childhood experiences of course can vary greatly, but there are some things that most people can understand or relate to: friends, teasing, movies, television, video games, crushes, sports, the arts, school, camp, work, smoking, drinking, drugs, bikes, skateboards, comic books, exploring nature, exploring the city, puberty, sex, embarrassment, science class, math class, English class, history class, rap music, rock music, country music, being bad, being good, parents, and adults.

I was born in 1978 at Stanford Hospital and spent my first eighteen years in a single house at the end of a cul-de-sac in Palo Alto. Palo Alto and its surrounding areas are some of the wealthiest in the country. They are the living grounds for all the dukes of Silicon Valley: Steve Jobs's daughter and the grandson of Hewlett (Hewlett-Packard) were both in my graduating class; our journalism teacher became the mother-in-law of one of the two Google founders. Considering the great amount of wealth and influence all around, Palo Alto is probably not a typical place to grow up. But I don't think that this stuff precludes it as a model.

Not only did I grow up among the children of the world shapers, but right across the 101 freeway was East Palo Alto, a separate city in a separate county that wasn't doing as well as Palo Alto. In fact, in 1992 it had the highest murder rate per capita in the country. It seems that the Palo Alto Police Department had a mandate to keep the crime from crossing over onto the wealthy side of the freeway, but that did not stop a certain amount of crossover. East Palo Alto didn't have its own high school because it was shut down, so the students were bused to other schools, including Palo Alto High School (Paly)—the students who were sent to Carlmont High School in Belmont inspired the book and film called *Dangerous Minds*. And East Palo Alto was one of the go-to places for Palo Alto teenagers to buy liquor and drugs. I'm not saying that this juxtaposition of two cities legitimates Palo Alto young people as subjects, or that anything in this situation was fair—I was just born into it; I didn't create it—but it shows that there was a diversity of experience within a small area.

I use childhood, teenagers, and school as forms. For me the particulars of the time and place of my own childhood are place-holders for anyone's experiences at that age. In my work, I show a more troubled side of young people in Palo Alto, not because I think the teenagers there are particularly bad, or because I think they are hard-off—far from it. I want to use them because I believe that all young people can be studied to access something more universal. When Nicholas Ray planned to make his own teenager piece, *Rebel Without a Cause*, he pointedly wanted his characters to live in nice suburbs—a definition of Palo Alto if I ever heard one—because he didn't want their actions to be explained away by economic consider-ations, as could be done with troubled-youth films set in inner cities. Maybe the teenagers in the 1950s didn't have a cause in the sense that they were rebelling against explicit oppression, but I think they were rebelling against the most insidious forces around: those of confor-mity and the capitalistic drive for monetary gain.

The young people of Palo Alto in the 1990s were in a similar position, except that social and pop influences were even more pervasive, so it is only more fitting to focus my work on the place that created so much of that other world that consumes half of our waking hours: cyberspace. These are kids trying to find themselves amid a hailstorm of cultural, scholastic, and—the most insidious of all—entertainment influences. In addition, this work was inspired by my own childhood. The text and images come from all periods of my artistic life, but the subject matter all derives from my younger years.

I'd make the claim that this is fiction, but what isn't nowadays?

me + Tom at
the downtown parade

Part I

Asilomar

Little Davy, Mom, Tom
          Dad + Me (Ted)

Betsy

me that Baby
Teddy

Drawing by tom,
age four?

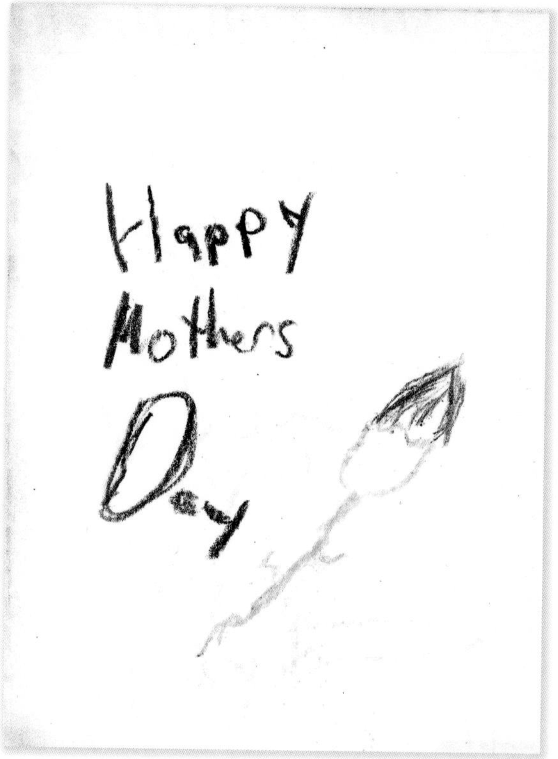
Happy
Mothers
Day

Mom's Diary

7/2/78 Doug and Ted really hit it off. Ted talks out loud a lot. He lies back in his bath.

9/24/78 The pace Teddy is learning now is pretty amazing. He can sit up pretty well, roll over and over, and he's starting to pick up some of the crawling movements. He's such a wiggleworm. He has an astonishing amount of energy. Thank goodness he goes down for 2 naps now.

10/28/78 Nicknames: Dukes, Dowkes, Dowkino, Dowkuner, Kino, Teddy Kino, Kino Kino, Puka, Fred, Ted the Fred, Teddo, Teddykins, Dowkuni Tedderkins, Ooks.

7/16/79 Teddy says: book, hi, dad, daddy, ball, mama, Teddy, no.

12/22/79 Teddy is very physical with his friends lately—hugging, tackling, jumping on them, wrestling.

2/20/80 Teddy loves his baseball hat. He wears it backwards. He can climb out of bed now. He did a backflip over the raised side of the crib.

I Love you

love,
Tolly

6/1/80 Teddy and I gave Tom a nice sponge bath and Tom peed on Teddy and we laughed.

6/28/80 Ted started fantasy play with make-believe food and make-believe trips to the duck pond. He says, "I love Mom. I love Dad. I love Tom."

8/20/80 Ted takes Tom to a pretend store for cookies. They lie on the floor. Ted calls Tom Old Seabag, darlin', honey, my little hamburger.

2/15/83 Teddy asked if George Washington was dead. Then he said, "Then why do we celebrate his birthday?"

2/15/83 Teddy told Tom that when kids say "Fuckerass" to him, he should say, "Not okay!"

5/18/87 Dave laughs all the time—he loves Tom and Ted.

3/8/88
When Ted whispers an answer to Davy, Davy whispers back:
Ted: What's 2 + 2?
Davy: Ummm
Ted (in a whisper): 4
Davy (in a whisper): 4

Back when it was
only me + Tom

young Davy

Mom + me at
the San Francisco Zoo

Tom and Me
at our shared
b-day party,
two + four.
Horrible hats.

High chair

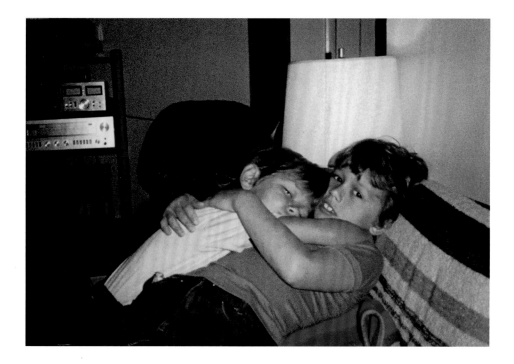

The old living room

Kindergarten

Kindergarten is a white room,
With colorful letters on the walls, high up.
Each letter is an animal,
O is for Ostrich, T is a Tiger.

In the middle of the floor is the green carpet
We all sit around, and sing.

My friend is Adam,
My first friend,
And Jewish.

There are girls
And everyone talks.
Kids have lots to say.

The girls draw rainbows,
The boys draw guns and helicopters.
I draw monsters with horns.

Madeline is the teacher, she's Vietnamese.
Miss Something comes and plays the oboe on Thursdays,
She puts a white glove on top and blows and it rises
and waves.

At Hanukkah we learn about Antiochus.
On the jungle gym no one wants to be Antiochus,
We all swing and battle Antiochus.
I can't ride a bike.
I go with the math kids and the Jewish kids to special places.
Some go to speech class, because they lisp.
We all learn writing,
T is the letter of my name,

And I write my name in a squiggly scrawl,
Which is me.

Girls go to the Girls,
Adam and I go to the Boys.
In the morning we pledge allegiance.
The flag droops on the pole, shy with its stars,
folding its stripes.

And all this is how the world is.

It could have been that blood wasn't blood,
but tigers,
And girls were oboes, and Madeline was a monster,
And we all floated, and didn't breathe air,

And I would be Antiochus.

Me + little Davy

The duck pond
at the baylands

artist in denim.
Light hair.

Drawings by all
the boys

First Grade

First grade with Mrs. Gong:
Well-ordered rows of desks.
We got points for right answers,
Pinar had the most by far.

I played a game with Eric and Angelo,
Pinching each other's balls.
Where it came from, I don't know.

We practiced cursive letters, repeated them on lines.
The letters formed words,
And we learned how the words
Become sentences.

Mrs. Gong saw our game.
She told our parents
And I stopped playing and began balling in earnest.

Second Grade

Mrs. D was Mrs. Donnely and I
Know that that means nothing to you
But to me it is a round woman
With a white bob and sharp nose
Like poultry parts.
And she was strict.

I fell in love for the first time.
Jenny Brown.
Adam Cohn loved her too.
One day we dissected fish,
And I thought of Adam when I took out the
Little guts and laid 'em on the tray like pebbles.

The smart kids could read whole books already.
They read *Charlotte's Web* and
The spider died.
But I couldn't read it yet,
I was still on the basics
Of sentences.

Jenny came over,
Our mothers were friends
And when the mothers left the room
We kissed.
Another time Jenny came over,
And I propped open the bathroom window,

And watched as she crouched
Girl-like on the toilet.
Jenny's father died when she was still little.
And soon after, Mrs. D died,
Like the spider.
I'm a sensitive pig, rooting in shit.

I want to be a Worker man

Talent show,
"Beat It"

New Mexico with our
cousin Bandi chorh

Domino!

Mom, the boys, and the old TV

strong man

The new living room

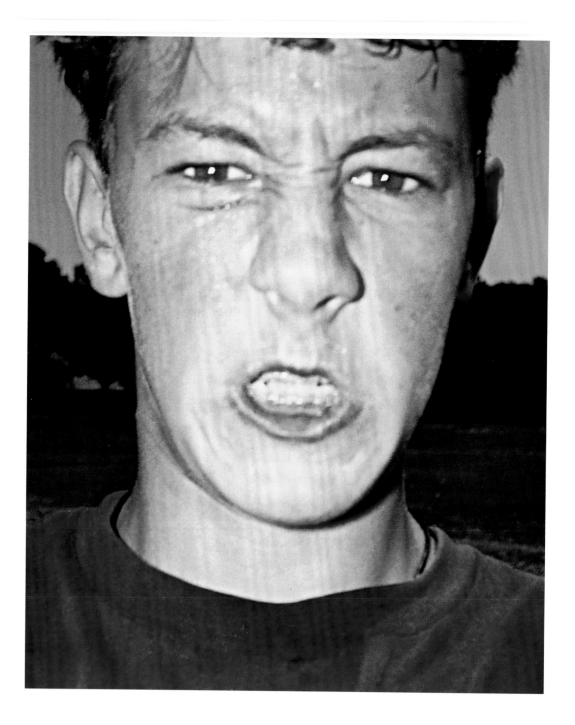

I got roller blades
for christmas
and only used them
for one day

Monster face

Eigth grade graduation,
me and Kasim

"Seventh grade" by me

My Place

I have a bucket on wheels and a mop, and sprays
For windows, toilets, and desks.
Children write things in all places.
Fuck you Ronny. For a good time call.

I'm supposed to wipe off all the graffiti,
Especially swastikas and racial slurs.

There is a hallway outside the math building
Full of faded brown lockers
Caged in with wire fencing.
Halfway down this hall
Is a door, and inside there, my place.

There is learning happening around me all day.
But sometimes I stay late when there are no more bells
Or voices. An orange frieze above the buildings,
Soon gray and then purple when the school lights turn on.

I can sit in my room all night if I wish.
There is an industrial sink and a chair
And I have papers and notes and receipts.
And a single bare bulb on a chain, so I can see.

Each morning I wash my hands and face
But it does no good.
When kids miss the toilet, I'm the one that cleans.
When it's clogged, I put my snake in there and clear it.

There is a faculty bathroom in the office building
—Called the Tower Building—
The one-unit bathroom is for staff only,
But students sneak in there and do it.

In my place there is complete privacy.
Not many are aware of it.
I keep the door closed.

When the kids are gone the school is a different place.
A shadow place. I'm a shadow.

I don't even look at the girls anymore. I love movies.
I watch them on my little portable.

Hilton Head
every summer

Karmann Ghia
with Grankpa and
bleached hair

Super Nintendo
with Davy

Hilton Head,
later days

Paddle ball

More Hilton
Head

Sophomore year.
Angry young Man.

Class of '95. They loved skiing,
the Beastie Boys, Soccer, and Water Polo.

"High School"
by
Josh Smith
&
James Franco

"Party Time"
by
Josh Smith
&
James Franco

Shannon. / Maurice.
She was wild. / He was bad.

Jamal.
Star athlete.
The plates on his purple
mercedes said, "PIMPIN."

"A-TEAM" / "The Dukes
of
HazzARD"
by
Josh Smith
&
James Franco

"Knight / "Uncle
RideR" / Jesse"

by
Josh Smith
&
James Franco

old painting

old painting

old Painting

old painting
"onward Ho"

JLS-Panthers
Jordan-Dolphins
Palo Alto Vikings
Gunn Titans
menlo

sike racks

JLS

re dy
1990

old painting
"schools"

old painting
"streets"

old Painting
"Riconada Pool"

Soccer

I wanted to write a poem about soccer.

I fucking hated it,
But it was something I did
Because my father liked it.

All the time,
He, my brother, and I would practice.
What a word, because I never got better;

No matter how much I tried,
I had friends who were better,
And I was like sniffly little Dedalus

On the side of the field, who gets
Pushed into the sewage.

I liked it much better in there,
It was something I could feel.

I wanted this poem to be about soccer.

I realize that if my dad taught me poetry
I would hate him for never teaching me
Soccer.

Dads have it rough,
They can't write poems for their sons.
I see now
All he could do
As a way of saying
I love you,
Was teach me to run stupidly around that field.

Wrestling

Leni Riefenstahl should look at this.
These muscles.
Actually, no, no muscles.

No, in this loose-fitting singlet,
There are no muscles.
No cock; no hair,
You're just a kid.

It turns out the best wrestler at Menlo-Atherton
Is in your weight class.
His weight is all muscle and yours is all
Not.

Those girls watching think you're cute
But they won't when you're on your back,
Pressed down by this beefcake,
Smiling white teethcake.

Fuck all these dads and people
That thought up this idea,
Greeks, fuck you too.

Plato didn't wrestle,
Socrates didn't fight.
You just want some hemlock,

Because this fucker's pits smell
And the mat is in your face,
And his muscles are tight
Around your neck and legs.

You're so in his control
You could melt into his skin,
And if this is life,

Life as a metaphor,
Where we all meet in a gym
And do this,
Then get out,
Get out and into something else.

Football

At practice,
Fifty calves flexing,
Making stuff happen in the mud,

This is how the world works,
This is what you're up against.

You'll never make it,
Your stomach is flabby,
And you don't know all the plays,

So when you quit
And they call you faggot,
They will be right.

Imagine the last minute
Of Super Bowl One Hundred:
It's tied,

A bunch of brutes
Lining up and smashing in the mud,
With cups over their cocks,
And their asses in tight pants.

So much invested in each body,
They no longer belong to the players.

This last minute of wills crashing,
Of money and entertainment,
Of corporate sponsorship,
Yes, exciting,

But I can't watch.
I never liked team sports.
I never liked sports,
Just the idea of them.

Josh Smith
+
James Franco

old painting
"Drinking"

old painting
"Friends"

Life Drawing Class,
I went every night my
Junior and senior years.

Jasmine

Jasmine.
We would listen to
live music at
St. Michael's Alley.

Jasmine in Hawaii.
I was on probation, so
my mom came with us.

Thinking about
art school

This past year my ambitions of becoming an artist have become a large part of my life. Two summers ago on a trip to Japan I was introduced to a man who influenced me to take art seriously. Up until then I had no resolve to do so. For the last year I have been taking life drawing courses outside of school.

Before my instructional courses I drew portraits of my family, in pastels mainly. These were mostly abstract and undisciplined. The actual drawing aspect of it thrilled me, but I usually got tired of the picture within a week. I wanted more discipline in my drawing, but I thought I was too young to take classes. There were courses at school, but they were reputed to be awful and lacked the instruction I desired. I continued to practice on my own whenever possible.

My grandmother deals Japanese art in Ohio, and often travels to Japan to visit the artists she represents. Two summers ago it was planned that I travel with my grandparents to Japan for a month. Of the artists I was introduced to there was one who attracted me. He lived in an old farmhouse in Kyoto with his wife and children. He was modest and kind but in his art he was total ambition. We were allowed to observe him paint. His work appeared almost systematic, as if he were revealing the picture he already saw on the canvas. Afterward he told me he began painting when he was my age and knew even then that it was what he was going to do. I dare say he was the one who got me serious about my art.

Last year I began taking life drawing classes, and during the summer I enrolled in a life drawing course at the Cleveland Institute of Art. There I received the thorough instruction I wanted. I began to see a definite direction for my art. I continue to take courses and practice outside of school. The courses I am taking can lead from painting to sculpture. I take it serious for I know in the future it may be the mode by which I express myself.

Grad night.
me, J.R. + Tenaya.

Childhood friend,
Jenny Brown

Woyzeck –
Killing my wife

6. In reading your application we want to get to know you as well as we can. We ask that you use this opportunity to tell us something more about yourself that would help us toward a sense of who you are, how you think, and what issues and ideas interest you most. Your statement should be done *in your own handwriting.* Be sure to sign at the bottom of page 4.

Late last spring, my father asked me to join him on a visit to Shree Maa, a meditation master living with her followers in Napa Valley. When we arrived, a group of 20 people were seated around an open fire, with the lead chanter singing quickly in Hindi. At given intervals, the group would chant a single "swaha" and throw rice into the fire. To the right sat a small Indian woman, and I knew immediately from her calm appearance that she was Shree Maa. To this day I can recall the soothing tone of her chanting. While listening to her, I became relaxed and all thoughts of my life in Palo Alto disappeared. My feelings of ease and freedom from worry fascinated me.

My father has been a practicing Hindu for ten years. But my own interest in Eastern religions was sparked by reading Herman Hesse's Siddhartha which portrays Siddhartha's path to enlightenment. After discussing Hesse's work with my father, I had reservations based on my understanding of the principal of intellect versus practice, which is essential to Buddhism. Hesse was not an accomplished meditator and was far from enlightenment. The authoritative way in which the book was written, as if it were revealing secrets about Buddhism, seemed a fallacy.

I began to approach the novel with strong skepticism, while other students embraced the book. At night my father and I continued to discuss Hinduism and Buddhism. I wrote a paper on the flaws I found in Siddhartha, and my teacher asked whether a novelist can write about ideas without direct experience of them. I would answer yes for subjects where experience is not pertinent, but on the topic of Buddhism and spirituality it goes against their very principals. Hesse contradicts the very thing he is writing about.

Shortly after writing my paper, I faced a dilemma similar to Hesse's. As a reporter/editor for my school newspaper, the Campanile, I decided to write an article on Buddhism to give other students information and expand my own knowledge. Yet, I was hesitant to write this feature because of my own criticisms of Hesse. My father suggested that I could write about Buddhism if I did not imply I was an authority, but rather admitted I was relaying information from people who possessed more advanced spiritual development.

My doubts about Hesse's novel and my own article represent the type of intellectual issue that interests me. This idea of theory versus practice is also evident in my pursuits as an artist and a journalist. This past summer, I studied life drawing at the Cleveland Institute of Art, and I continue to draw from models in classes outside of school. This practice requires hands-on experience in contrast to the observer role I have as a journalist. Bringing together and reconciling these different approaches is the kind of challenge I expect to find in college.

Palo Alto High School

Guidance Office

94306-2387 BB

Ted,
Really good job.
—Dad.

PALO ALTO
CALIF.
NOV 17 '94

METER
6029828

US POSTAGE
0.29

COURSE	MK	CREDIT	COURSE	MK	CREDIT	COURSE	MK	CREDIT	COURSE	MK	CREDIT	ENROLLMENT HISTORY
PALO ALTO HIGH SCH			PALO ALTO HIGH SCH			PALO ALTO HIGH SCH						EL CARMELO ELEM SCHOOL
GRD 09 SEM 01/93			GRD 10 SEM 06/94			GRD 12 SEM 01/96						PALO ALTO, CA
EXP THNK 1*	C+	5.00	CHEMIST 1A*	C-	5.00	CUM CR GPA CUR GPA						DATES 09/12/83-06/14/90
WLD HIST *	A	5.00	JAPANES 3 *	B+	5.00	255.00 3.33 3.67						STANFORD MIDDLE SCH
GEOM A *	B-	5.00	AUTO TECH	B	5.00							PALO ALTO, CA
FOOTBALL	A	0.00	CUM CR GPA CUR GPA			CUM STATE GPA 3.41						DATES 09/04/90-06/13/91
PE	A	5.00	140.00 2.96 2.71									JORDAN MIDDLE SCH
BIOLOGY 1 *	C-	5.00				* = UNIV OF CA PREP						PALO ALTO, CA
JAPANES 2 *	B	5.00	PALO ALTO HIGH SCH			CA ST UNIV PREP						DATES 09/03/91-06/12/92
YRBOOK	B	5.00	GRD 11 SEM 01/95			** = CA ST UNIV ONLY						PALO ALTO HIGH SCH
CUM CR GPA CUR GPA			AM CLAS11H*	A-	5.00							PALO ALTO, CA
35.000 3.00 3.00			ADV JOURN *	A	5.00	MINIMUM COMPETENCY						DATES 09/08/92-PRESENT
			US HIST *	A	5.00	MATH COMP PASSED						
PALO ALTO HIGH SCH			AB CALC AP*	A	5.00	MATH APPL PASSED						
GRD 09 SEM 06/93			PE 11	A	5.00	READ COMP PASSED						
CRIT THNK1*	C	5.00	COLBIOL AP*	A-	5.00	WRITING PASSED						
WLD HIST *	A-	5.00	JAPANES 4 *	B	5.00	RD-WRT APPL PASSED						
GEOM A *	C	5.00	CUM CR GPA CUR GPA			# = NOT PASSED						
BIOLOGY 1 *	B-	5.00	175.00 3.14 3.86									
JAPANES 2 *	B+	5.00				SUBJ REQ'D SHORT						
YRBOOK	B	5.00	PALO ALTO HIGH SCH			ECON 5.00 5.00						
LIV SKILL	A-	5.00	GRD 11 SEM 06/95									
CUM CR GPA CUR GPA			HUMAN 11H *	A	5.00							
70.000 3.00 3.00			CR WRIT 11*	A-	5.00							
			ADV JOURN *	A	5.00							
PALO ALTO HIGH SCH			US HIST *	A	5.00							
GRD 10 SEM 01/94			AB CALC AP*	A	5.00							
CRIT THNK2*	B	5.00	COLBIOL AP*	A	5.00							
CONTWLD 11*	B-	5.00	JAPANES 4 *	B+	5.00							
PRE CALC *	B	5.00	CUM CR GPA CUR GPA									
PE 10/11	A	5.00	210.00 3.26 3.86									CSF 94-95 SEM 1
CHEMIST 1A*	C-	5.00										
JAPANES 3 *	B+	5.00	PALO ALTO HIGH SCH									
AUTO TECH	A	5.00	GRD 12 SEM 01/96									
CUM CR GPA CUR GPA			COL ENG AP*	B	5.00							
105.00 3.05 3.14			WLDCLAS11H	A-	5.00							COUNSELORS
			ADV JOURN *	A	5.00							FIRST AID REQ MET 92
PALO ALTO HIGH SCH			SOC 11 *	A-	5.00							
GRD 10 SEM 06/94			BC CALC AP*	B	5.00							
CRIT THNK2*	B	5.00	PE 10/11	A	5.00							CERTIFIED DATE
JOURNAL 11*	B+	5.00	PHYSICS 1H*	A	5.00							3.11.96
US GOVT *	B	5.00	ARTHIST AP	B	5.00							
PRE CALC *	C+	5.00	EXPL EXP11	A	5.00							

Grades

Mom

Dad

At the airport,
going to college

Senior boys Calendar,
"The Thinker"

Part II

Yearbook Staff,
Freshman year

Camp

We all went to the camp.

We were twelve and thirteen years old. Me and Ivan and Howard and Ute and Ed. Jewish, Russian, Jewish, Italian, and half Korean/ half white. I had turned thirteen in April.

It was a YMCA water ski camp. There were a husband and wife who ran everything, but the husband was the head counselor. The husband had well-manicured dark hair and a clipped beard that fit his face; the wife had blond hair to her shoulders. He was in his forties, and she looked younger. A pleasant, Christian-looking mom and dad.

He wore a tan explorer's hat with a floppy brim and a string that hung down under his chin. His wife did the roll call and made sure everybody was where they should be. They both led the songs around the campfire at night, but she led more of them. Sometimes he would play his guitar. We sang many different songs, and sometimes the husband told ghost stories. It sounded like he had told the stories a million times but that he was trying to make them exciting each time. I think he was very proud of them and thought they were good just because he had told them so many times. At the end we always sang "The Lion Sleeps Tonight."

It was so dirty around the fire, and I'd always get smoke in my mouth.

We were too old for the camp.

Jane was our counselor even though we were all boys. She was the daughter of the head counselor and his wife. Jane had blond hair like her mom. Later she told us that she was the black sheep of her family.

Another counselor was Hulk.

Hulk was very tall and big, like a bulky potato shape, fat but really strong. He had huge calves that were red from the sun because he wore shorts all the time. His shorts hung to his fat knees, and he had them in all ugly colors, like pink, and they were dirty and worn from the woods. Or fluorescent orange with swirl designs, or cutoff denim. He wore big brown Timberland boots without tying the laces. He had a curly mullet and a goatee, and he wore Vuarnet sunglasses. The Vuarnets were a single lens that went across both eyes and reflected rainbows in the sunlight.

Ed and I had had him for a counselor the first time when we were eight. That was for a different camp in a different set of woods, but Hulk was the same then.

Howard was Jewish, and I was Jewish because my mom was Jewish. I never went to Hebrew school, but I was circumcised.

When I was a kid my friend Nick and I made a potion together. Nick was French; his dad had a pointy beard and spoke with an accent. We got a big rectangular plastic tub and put snails in it and red pyracantha berries, which were poisonous and made the black-birds drunk so they flew into the windows and died. And we took cat poo from the sandbox with a plastic shovel and put it in the soup. At the end we peed in it. My penis was like a mushroom, and my French friend's was draped in skin, like a monk's cowl.

We tried to get my little brother to drink it, but he wouldn't. We left our potion in the backyard in the rectangular tub. One day I found a dead rat next to it.

In fourth grade Mr. DeFelice was my teacher. He was younger than all the other teachers. He said his name meant he was always happy. He told us he ate pizza and drank beer at Luigi's in Mountain View. That was the next city over, but far for me. He said he was good at *Top Gun* on Nintendo. He could get to the space level. A jet in space doesn't make sense.

In ninth grade we watched a lot of Holocaust stuff. We saw pictures and then a film of the naked bodies being bulldozed. Penises on the men and vaginas and breasts on the women. They didn't seem like real penises. I looked close. Some were big.

I had a cat named Toby. He was put to sleep at the vet's. Gassed? Buried? Incinerated. Way of all flesh and fur.

Ed was at my very first Y camp when we were eight. He was half Korean from his mom, and his dad was a big, white, bald dork. One morning Hulk took us to the lake. It was so cold. We had our towels around our shoulders. Mine was *The Incredible Hulk*; Ed had *The Dukes of Hazzard*. There was a Confederate flag on the side of their car.

Hulk said we were all in the Polar Bear Club. He was the whale of the club.

We took our shirts off. Nobody had muscles. Hulk said he would give a Coke to whoever went in the lake naked.

One night in ninth grade we were drunk and wandering around the neighborhoods in a pack. There were some girls with us too. There was nowhere to go and no more alcohol.

We walked through Mid-Peninsula, the school for bad kids who got kicked out of other schools. They were allowed to smoke cigarettes during their brunch break. They were mostly white, and they wore a lot of black. One year a kid brought a gun to school and shot his ex-girlfriend at brunch because she had a new boyfriend. Then he shot the new boyfriend. Then he shot himself. The girl didn't live, but the new boyfriend lived.

We never had any black friends. Not before high school and not in high school. But we liked black rappers. Dr. Dre, 2Pac, DJ Quik, Too $hort, and the Geto Boys.

At water ski camp there was a black girl, Angela. She had no friends at camp because she was weird. She would talk about aliens. She said she and her brothers saw aliens, but it sounded like her brothers were her only friends and that her brothers were the ones who came up with the alien idea.

We dared Howard to make out with her in the back of the bus. He did one night. On the way back to the campsite he kissed her, but it was messy, like two lizards. We were in the seat in front of them, and we saw him feel her small breasts, and under the towel he felt her vagina. We looked back and saw it all. It was a purple towel with nothing on it. He was the first of us to do all that, but it was with the black alien girl.

I had my first girlfriend in fourth grade, in Mr. DeFelice's class. Her name was Simone. She was pretty and blond like Madonna. After she broke up with me I would watch *Who's That Girl* to remind myself of her. Once Simone said Mr. DeFelice asked if he could take pictures of her at his house, but her mom wouldn't let her go.

Ute's name was the name of an Indian tribe. He was Italian, but his parents were hippies and accountants at Whole Foods. His older brother was named Rain, and he was two years older than us. Rain had the biggest dick of all his friends. He would walk around naked showing it, and all his friends talked about it. They called him "Calcium."

Calcium broke all the baseball records in high school and had sex with tons of ugly girls.

Later, in high school, Ute had sex first out of all of us. It was with a black girl, Venus.

I had sex last. I was drunk at a party at my friend Barry's house. We did it in a bedroom, Susan and me, and then stayed the night. In the morning, I waited till she left, and then I walked home alone.

At water ski camp we told everyone about Howard and the black girl on the bus. There was a handsome guy, Chad. He got into a fight with Howard and punched him in the eye. Chad didn't get in trouble because he told the counselors about what Howard did to Angela.

After I had sex once I had sex a lot. The second time was in Susan's bed. I was about to come and I pressed my foot against the foot-board. My long toenails scraped against the board like cockroaches. After, when we pulled away, it was sticky and frothy. Buttery, like pulling apart a Baby Ruth.

She rolled over and cried.

When I was eight, we all loved Coke. The bright red can with the cold brown liquid. There was one machine back at the main counselor's cabin. If we did something good, we got a can.

Everybody in the Polar Bear Club wanted a Coke. But no one wanted to get naked in front of Hulk. Hulk took his shirt off. He was fat and pale and had hair on the front of his shoulders. His stomach was like curdled milk. There were little chunks of ill-formed fat that showed through the skin when he moved. The skin on his stomach was as white as the inside of a radish.

In fourth grade, in Mr. DeFelice's class, I had to sit next to Sasha Alexander. She wore the thickest glasses I've ever seen. She had short red hair, lots of freckles, and no friends.

The class practiced writing cursive. We had to write our desk partner's name. Mr. DeFelice came around to inspect. He told me my *x* in *Alexander* looked like a swastika.

In eleventh grade we studied the Civil War. There were the Bad Confederates and the Good Guys in the North. Some people still believe that the Confederates were right.

The water ski camp went to Knott's Berry Farm. Ute and Howard and I and the others weren't allowed to go into Knott's Berry Farm because of the fight Howard had with Chad and because of what Howard did with the black girl and because he told that we had made him do it. The head counselor and his wife wanted to kick us out of camp, but instead we missed out on Knott's Berry Farm. It was Hulk's idea. We stayed in the parking lot by the bus with Jane and threw a Frisbee. Jane had to stay because she was our counselor.

She was sad for us. That was when she told us that she was the black sheep of the family.

At the very end of the day we got to go into Knott's Berry Farm. We saw Chad. He had his T & C tank top on. He had met a local girl in the park. His friend told us that Chad had got to second base with her already when they went on the mine ride. She was blond and pretty.

Riding back to the campsite, Ute drew pictures of people being burned in ovens. He burned Howard and Chad and Hulk in his ovens. They went in as they were—Ute was good at drawing cartoons, so it actually looked like them—and they came out as skeletons.

A little kid told about the drawings. Hulk came back and saw the pictures. Back at camp he told us how bad the Nazis were and that it was not something to joke about.

Nobody in the camp liked us.

Ute was handsome, but he was a nerd too. He drew lots of pictures. Ed and I drew pictures with him. We made our own comic called *The Alien Brothers*. We drew ourselves like vicious aliens and killed the people in our school.

In fourth grade Sasha Alexander was the biggest dork I could ever think of. Buckteeth and short red hair and glasses. She said she could play basketball better than me. I laughed. We played at lunch and I won. She didn't admit that I won. Back in class I told her she was a dork and a poor loser, and she stabbed me in the arm with a pencil. The hole was gray from the graphite.

Mr. DeFelice didn't do anything about it.

When we were eight this guy pulled Ed's bathing suit off. Ed didn't
have a mushroom. He was half Korean. We were scared to fight the
big guy who did it. Hulk didn't know about it, so the kid didn't get
in trouble.

In high school it was mostly white kids. There were only about thirty
black students. Some were bused in from East Palo Alto. Most of
them hung out in an area in front of the school library. That was
their spot. They got bad grades and wore parkas.

The night at Mid-Pen we were drunk and tired of walking. Ivan and
Ed and Jack and I stood on the cement-filled tire of a tetherball pole.
We held the pole and rocked the tire back and forth and sang songs.
The rest of the group left, except for Ute, who stood there and pouted.

    We were drunk, and we came up with our own songs. We sang
about Heebs, and stingy Jews. Not meanly, just loud and funny. I
sang loud.

    Ute was mad about it. He asked how we could do that to Dave
Frankel and Howard, and he left. No one cared. We didn't care about
Howard; he was a fool.

At water ski camp we made fun of Howard and the black girl,
Angela, so much. Late at night we snuck out of our sleeping bags and
smoked pot. At campfire one night we dared Howard to push Angela
in the water.

    We sang "Wimoweh, wimoweh," and then as everyone walked
back to their sleeping bags, Howard shoved her in. She had all her
clothes on. She hit her tooth on a log.

    We got kicked out.

In high school Ute had so much pressure from his brother, Rain, to have sex. His brother made fun of him, and would get him drunk, and rip off his clothes, and tie him up. Ute finally had sex with Venus. The black guys made fun of Ute and Venus. They all wanted Venus.

The football players like Sam liked to make fun of Jews. He called people "Heebs" when they "Jewed" him. Sam played center on the team. He was fat and got no girls. He drank a lot of beer. Dave Frankel was Jewish and was on the team. He didn't say anything to Sam about all his talk.

In history our teacher, Mr. Tyson, did a reenactment of the Anne Frank story. It was an elaborate thing that he did every year. He staged it on top of the machine shop in the storage room. He made the storage room look like Anne Frank's attic. It was very fancy. Students played the Franks. At the end Mr. Tyson busted through the door dressed like an SS agent. He was pretty convincing.

When they kicked us out of camp, Hulk drove us to the Greyhound bus station in the middle of the night. Howard cursed at him the whole way. He called him a child molester and a little-dicked faggot. Hulk didn't say anything. Howard kept going for the whole ride; it took about an hour. Howard's face was red by the end. Whenever Hulk switched gears, Howard told him to "work that stick."

At the Greyhound station in Redding, Hulk bought us all tickets and put us on the bus. He watched as we drove off. I saw him walk away before the bus was out of sight.

Then we were in the dark bus with the real people, traveling in the middle of the night. Most of the people were Mexican, and were sleeping. We were all quiet; there was nothing left to do.

There was a layover in Sacramento. We got out and wandered around. There was a seedy hotel near the station called the Henderson Hotel. It made us think of a slut at our school called Alice Henderson, and we laughed about it. They sold hot dogs and beer in the lobby. The guy behind the counter said that Axl Rose had stayed there once.

It was one in the morning.

When we went back to the depot, Ed and I had both lost our ticket receipts and we couldn't get on the bus. The woman in the customer service booth told us to go talk to the driver.

We went around to the side of the depot where the drivers had their lounge. Through the small window in the door we could see them. They were all black guys, sitting in there laughing and drinking coffee out of blue-and-white Styrofoam cups. They looked like they were having such a good time.

JV Volleyball

Meredith at
sushi place
in TSC

Freaks

Peter Parker

He walked along the sidewalk in the hot sun. It was afternoon. Now that he was in first grade, Joe was allowed to go as far as the pharmacy on Middlefield in one direction, and the busy street, Alma, in the other. He used to go to the pharmacy, Midtown Pharmacy, every day. A nice Chinese man worked behind the counter. But Joe hadn't gone back since they found the gum in his pocket. That was when he met Brad.

Joe used to go into the pharmacy and sit on the floor and read *Spider-Man.*

Peter Parker was Spider-Man.

One day, the fat man with the red face was working. He worked when the Chinese man, Mr. Lim, wasn't there. The fat man with the red face told Joe to empty his pockets. Joe was sitting on the floor; he stood up and emptied his pockets. His jeans were tight, so it was hard to pull the pockets out. When he pulled them all out, a piece of Bazooka bubble gum fell on the floor. Joe said it was his, but the fat man said it wasn't. Brad was there. Brad said he would pay for it, but the fat man told Joe never to come back again.

Brad was old, but not as old as Joe's dad. When the fat red-faced man told Joe to leave, Brad followed Joe outside. Brad was smiling. He had black hair and wore a brown T-shirt that said HÄGGEN-DAZS. He told Joe he had lots of comic books at his house. He lived near the high school. That was farther than Joe was allowed to go. The high school was in the other direction, past Alma.

Brad said that if he came over he would give Joe a ride home after.

At Brad's house there were lots of comic books. Brad told him to pick one to read. He had a lot of old ones in plastic. Joe picked

Spider-Man, and Brad pulled it out of the plastic. Joe sat on the couch, and Brad went into the kitchen.

"Are you just looking at the pictures?" Brad said when he came back. He had two Cokes. Joe couldn't read yet, a little, but not much. Not like Manuel, whose parents were strict. Manuel could read when he was four.

Brad sat on the couch next to Joe and read to Joe what the words in the bubbles said. Joe looked at the pictures. It was fun to hear what Spider-Man was saying. Brad was good at it. They drank the Cokes, and it was pretty fun. Then Joe said he had to go home and Brad drove him.

At home it was quiet. Joe sat on his own couch and watched TV. The house was bad since his dad left. And it was bad before that, when his brother, Tim, died of spinal meningitis that he got from his kindergarten teacher, Miss Brown. She died too. Tim went to bed early one night because he was feeling sick, and he never woke up. Joe's dad was supposed to be watching him, but he was in the garage listening to his music. In the garage he had Budweiser and Camel cigarettes. After, his dad didn't drink beer anymore, but it was too late. His mom hated his dad.

Joe got in trouble at school. He and Manuel played a game where they tried to pinch each other's privates. It wasn't a game they made up; it just happened. Manuel did it to him, so he did it back. After that they would pinch or twist the other one whenever they could. He didn't like playing, but he didn't know how to stop it, because it just kept going and going. Mrs. Ming caught them when Manuel did it really hard to Joe. Joe was working on his handwriting pages and screamed really loud. They both went outside with Mrs. Ming, and Joe was crying. Not because he was hurt but because he was going to get in trouble. Mrs. Ming asked what the game was, but she already knew. She told them not to talk to each other. Manuel's parents said Joe couldn't play at Manuel's house anymore.

Joe had no one to play with. Then he figured out how to get to Brad's house. It was near the high school, and that was near the train tracks. He started going every day. He was going again.

He walked toward Alma, the busy street. The sun was hot, and he walked quickly. He sucked on a lollipop. It was purple. He bit it, and pieces stuck in his molars. He got to Alma and waited. He stood on one foot and then the other, then he crossed the busy street. He was like the frog in the video game *Frogger*. His dad let him play it at his work at IBM the one time Joe went. That was before his dad didn't work anymore, and before Tim died.

No cars hit him going across the street. On the other side, he ducked through the wall of oleander bushes. His mom taught him the name. They were poison to eat. They had sticky milky leaves. It got sticky on his hands and face.

Behind the bushes were the train tracks. They went far in both directions. The sun was even hotter there. The heat was on the white and gray stones that were around the tracks. They were sharp stones.

He took off his shoes and socks and put his socks into his blue Nikes with the white swoosh symbol. He tied the laces together in a bow and hung them over his right shoulder. Joe stepped between the train track ties, onto the pointy rocks. He wanted his feet to get tough. The rocks were hot, and they poked the bottoms of his feet in the middle, where they were sensitive. He wouldn't tell anyone he did that. Not even Brad. He swore to God that he wouldn't tell anyone. Just like he swore that he would never tell the joke about black people that his babysitter Marissa told him.

He believed in God. When he prayed at night, he said he loved God more than his mom and dad. His cat died, and he was with God. He didn't say goodbye to Stoney. His mom took him to the vet, and then he was gone. They put him to sleep.

That night he cried all night, and his father came home late. It was when his dad lived at home, after he had stopped drinking beer, but before he left. He stood next to Joe's bunk bed. Joe was in the top, curled up, and no one was in the bottom because Tim was dead. Joe cried when his brother died, but not as much as when Stoney died. His dad told him that it was okay, cats died all the time.

"Joey, when Grandpa was a kid, he drowned a whole bag of kittens in the bathtub."

That made Joe cry more. Why did Grandpa drown all the kittens? And where did he put them after?

He walked down the tracks. People died on train tracks. Sometimes his father told him about being a kid in Chicago. He said it was much worse than Palo Alto.

When his dad was a kid, there was a woman who got hit by a train. When people are hit by trains, his dad said, sometimes they bounce off the train and they're dead, and sometimes they explode. This woman exploded.

Two boys that his father knew went to the tracks and picked up pieces of the woman and put them into a paper grocery bag. They brought the bag to school and showed the pieces to all the kids.

What pieces were they? His father couldn't remember. Little pieces.

When Joe got a scab, he could pick the scab off, and it would be a little piece of him that was separated from him. Once his friend Manuel gave him a scab from his knee, from skateboarding. Joe kept it in his jeans pocket, but it got lost in the dryer. He could have swallowed it, and Manuel would have been inside him, like a little baby.

Joe had a scab on his elbow. He could sneak it into someone's food. Then he would be inside someone and they wouldn't know. He could do that to his babysitter Marissa. He picked it off. It bled.

His mom left for weekends to go to writer conferences, and Marissa would babysit him. She was sixteen and Israeli. She talked to boys out in the front yard when it was dark. It was weird that they were on his front lawn because he didn't know them but they were on his lawn. He saw them from the big window. They were out in the dark, smoking cigarettes.

Like his dad's friends who smoked cigarettes at the big AA picnics. Everyone had tattoos at the picnics. Dragons and skeletons and snakes.

At one picnic, Joe was watching a softball game. It was very hot, and there were lots of people with their shirts off. They were watching too. Then it felt like someone pinched him, but very sharp. He saw a cigarette in a man's hand. The man didn't know he had burned Joe. He had long hair and dragons and writing on his wrinkly, tan arms. Then the man looked at Joe. He had big glasses on that were one single lens and said VUARNET. He smiled at Joe.

"Oh, did I sting ya?"

Joe said nothing.

"You're John H.'s son, right?"

He was.

"Ya look like him," he said. Most of the man's teeth were yellow. On the tracks in the distance Joe saw a train. There were two sets of tracks. It was on his track. He was walking on the left track, and the train was coming at him. Trains go on the right side like cars.

Someone coming at you has their right side on the other side. So the train was on his track. He waited for a little to let the train get closer. Then he walked quickly to the side. It hurt his feet because he was running fast on the rocks. There was spray paint on the wall next to the tracks. It was a picture of a sad ghost, and underneath it said ORFN.

The train was coming, and he waited. It got bigger and louder. The engine was gray.

One time he put a penny on the tracks with Marissa. After the trains passed, the pennies came out flat and smooth. But someone told Marissa it was dangerous because they can shoot into your eye.

At school Mrs. Ming told him and Manuel a story. She said in China, two boys were fighting, and one boy put a spoon in the other boy's eye, and his eye slipped out. Just like a little fish, she said.

The train was there, and it was all there was, noise and motion. It rushed past, and the windows on the side became one window, and there were heads in the window. Faces, looking and reading. Then the back caught up and passed. There was no caboose. It got quieter. Then there was the sound of cars again, driving on Alma on the other side of the oleander bushes.

There was a muddy puddle by the wall where he stood, but no frogs. There used to be frogs in his backyard when his dad lived there. They would put them in the little plastic pool and put big rocks in the pool for the mommy and daddy frogs and the baby frogs to play on. He would hold them, and they would pee on him, because they were scared. But they didn't come in the backyard anymore.

One time, at the end before his dad left, he and his dad tried to make frogs from tadpoles. They went with plastic cups to Lake Lagunita and hunted for tadpoles. They caught a bunch, and the big ones they called daddy tadpoles, and the little ones they called mommy tadpoles, and they took them home in the plastic cups that had lake water in them, and he had to hold the cups very carefully in the car, so that the tadpoles didn't spill out.

His dad bought a medium-sized aquarium and filled it with plants and water, and they put all the tadpoles in it. The tadpoles were supposed to eat the plants, but instead they ate each other. At the end there was only one big tadpole, with two legs at the back, and it swam around alone and never turned into a frog. His mom made him put it in the toilet.

One time he and his dad watched that movie about the baby alligator that went into the toilet and then got big and ate everyone.

A little way down he could see cars crossing over the tracks. That was the street where the high school was, and Brad's house. He turned off the tracks onto the street called Churchill. His feet felt better on the sidewalk than on the rocks. There were some older kids leaving the high school. Two boys and one girl. One was walking a bike.

At the end of the block and around the corner was Brad's house with a little brown fence, shorter than he was. Behind it was a blue house with peeling paint and white trim. Brad was there in a red T-shirt. He was on the porch smoking a cigarette.

"Hey, bud," said Brad. Then he said, "Your shoes are off."

"I'm thirsty," said Joe.

"You want a Coke?"

"Some water first."

"Here, drink from the hose." The hose was in the grass by some plants. There wasn't any nozzle at the end, and the water was coming out and soaking into the dirt. They both walked over to the hose.

The grass was long and overgrown and soft under Joe's feet. Brad picked up the hose and held it out in Joe's direction, and the water splashed on his feet.

Joe used to kill ants on his front porch with a hose. So many ants. He would pour the water into the cracks of the porch, and they would float away. But the ants kept coming out.

"Drink," said Brad.

Joe leaned over a little and drank from the stream of water. It was cool and tasted thick, like it was from under the earth. It splashed on his face and made his lips and the area around his mouth wet. A little got in Joe's nose and made him think of swimming.

One time at the beach, his dad pulled Tim's arm out of the socket when he was playing airplane.

Brad dropped the hose, and the water spilled into the grass. They went into the house.

"Now you want a Coke?" said Brad. Joe did.

Brad was close and smelled strong. Brad walked into the kitchen to get the Cokes, and Joe went to pick a comic book. He picked *Spider-Man*, number 7. There was a bald birdman called The Vulture flying over Spider-Man.

"How was school?" Brad said from the kitchen.

"I got in trouble."

"Why?"

Brad came back with the cold Cokes, and Joe told him that it was about Manuel. Manuel had begun playing the game again. Manuel did it once when Mrs. Ming wasn't looking, then he did it again. Mrs. Ming didn't see that, but she saw Joe trying to stab Manuel with his pencil. Then she told them about the boy who lost his eye.

"It can happen," said Brad. "Eyes come out pretty easily."

"I wish I was Peter Parker so I could be Spider-Man," said Joe.

"I'll call you Peter Parker if you want me to."

"Okay."

Then Brad said, "You know, privates are your own special place. No one is supposed to touch them if you don't want them to."

They sat on the couch, and Brad read the words, and Joe looked at the pictures. He pretended he was Peter Parker.

His father used to read to him. Around the time that Tim died, he stopped working at IBM. He stayed at the house. He wore a kimono and sat in the garage and smoked cigarettes and listened to music on his headphones and drank beer. There were big trash bags full of his beer cans next to the garbage bins by the side of the house.

"My dad reads to me too sometimes," said Joe.

"Oh yeah? But he's in San Jose, right?"

Yeah, he was across the freeway in San Jose. Joe saw him once every two weeks.

Sitting next to Brad, it was the smell of his dad, like a yellow smell, like the yellow of the Camel on the cigarette boxes in the garage.

"What's the game with Manuel?" said Brad.

"It's not a game," said Joe.

"But what do you do to each other?" asked Brad. Joe didn't want to do it to Brad.

"Does he do this?" Brad acted like he was doing it, but didn't touch Joe. Joe nodded, yes, that was what Manuel did.

"And what do you do?" said Brad. Joe just sat there. Then he showed him without touching.

"Well, you shouldn't do that with Manuel if you don't want to."

"I don't want to."

"Good."

They looked at the comic book and said nothing.

"You'll come back, right?"

"Yes," said Joe.

They were still just looking at the comic book.

"I like when you come over."

"Me too."

"I don't want you to get in trouble for crossing Alma."

"I won't tell."

When he left at five he asked Brad for a lollipop. This one was cherry.

"Can I try your cigarette?" said Joe.

"Maybe next time. Just watch out for bad guys, okay, Peter?"

He walked home on the train tracks, but he had his shoes on now. He would wait till tomorrow to build up his calluses. It wasn't hot going back. The oleander bushes were making shadows. At the right spot he crawled through. A few cars slowed for him on Alma as he crossed back.

Ivan.
my friend.
He was bad.
Jumped off a building
after high school.

The Deer

I always sat in the back of Mr. Kim's algebra class. He was very
enthusiastic about algebra. I drew a picture of me sticking my dick
into Rex's blond dream girl. Rex was on the other side of the room.
I folded the paper and wrote *Rex* on the top, and told this ugly girl,
Andrea Blatt, to pass it along. She passed it to another girl who
passed it, and everyone passed it until it got to Rex. He couldn't tell it
was supposed to be his dream girl. He laughed out loud. Mr. Kim
looked at him, and then looked at me. People tell me I look like
Warren Beatty; maybe that's why he was staring.

We went out and got croissants and cold chocolate milk in little
cartons. We discussed our Santa Cruz trip. Seth Cranston was with
us. In eighth grade we called him "Naps." Then one day, this white
kid we didn't know called him Naps, and Seth beat the kid into a
coma. Seth went to juvenile hall. While he was in there, he stabbed
another kid with a pencil seventeen times, and it was in the *Palo Alto
Weekly*. Finally he got out. No one called him Naps anymore.

We were all across the street at Town & Country, in the parking
lot where everyone smokes if they're not smoking in the bat cave. I
have a brown 1987 Buick LeSabre station wagon. My dad gave it to
me. It's a boat with a thin plastic steering wheel and a faux-wood dash.
It is as slow as a cloud. My dad is rich, but he's cheap. All the little
skaters were around, smoking and doing ollies. Seth heard our Santa
Cruz plan, and he asked if he could go. We said no, it was a private
thing. Seth was pissed. He stood up and pushed one of the skaters off
his board. Seth got on the board and did a bad ollie on it. Then he rode
it into the street and jumped off. It broke under a car's wheels on
Embarcadero. The kid whose board it was called Seth Naps. I choked

on my chocolate milk. Seth walked over to the kid. All the kid's friends backed away. They all had wide eyes. Rex and I sat on the curb, watching and laughing. I had this thick, coated feeling in my throat from the chocolate milk, the Camel cigarettes, and the rest of the croissant I was chewing on, and I was still a little high.

The little skater had long black bangs that hung straight down in front. He wore a skater outfit: baggy pants and a baggy black T-shirt. For a second, the kid was trying to act tough, but Seth grabbed him by his bangs in the front and pulled his face downward so he was bending over. The kid grabbed Seth's hand and was kicking at Seth, but he couldn't reach. Then Seth whipped the kid's head up and back in a violent jerk. The kid was almost crying. There was nothing he could do because Seth was so much bigger. Then the kid fell on his ass, but Seth was still holding his bangs. The kid was sitting there, holding Seth's hand and screaming, and Seth was stepping on the kid's stomach, and then on his neck and face, while still pulling his bangs. Rex and I were dying because the kid was pulling at Seth's leg to make him stop and he started pulling off Seth's sweatpants, and it was making Seth madder. Seth was telling the kid to stop pulling off his pants. Then Seth's tightie-whities were showing and they looked yellow.

The driver that ran over the skateboard pulled into the parking lot. He was in this stupid brown station wagon, just like mine. He started yelling at Seth to stop, and we all yelled back at him. We told him to get in the car and to get the fuck out of there. Even the other little skaters were yelling at him. The only one not yelling at him was the kid on the ground because he was still struggling with Seth. Then Rex and I threw our chocolate milk at the car. The driver got back in his car and said he was going to call the police.

We all went back to class.

I had biology third period. We were dissecting piglets. It was sick. My partner was Meena Cohen. She screeched when I cut open the piglet. I cut off the pig's head, even though I wasn't supposed to, and she screeched a whole bunch more. There were a lot of screeches all over the room, so Meena wasn't alone.

Right after I cut off the pig's head, Simpson came by, on his stupid bicycle. He was security on campus. Assistant football coach. He told Ms. Johnson that he was taking me to the office. I was holding the pig head by the ear when Ms. Johnson told me to go with Simpson. I walked out with the head behind my back. We walked across the lawn. Simpson was walking his mountain bike and his big ass in his little shorts. I dropped the pig head in the bushes before we went up the office steps. I didn't get in trouble. Seth got suspended. Dean Schneiderman told me I was mean-spirited for laughing at the skater's pain. By the time I got out, fourth period was half over. Simpson was gone. I grabbed the pig head out of the bushes. It had some dirt on the cut neck. I went over to the spot between the theater and the office, where nobody goes. I smoked three cigarettes. I put the cigarettes out on the pig's eyelids. He looked angry. Then it was lunch.

At lunch we all went over to Terry Price's. I saw him walking to the parking lot, and he told me to come over. I drove over in my brown LeSabre. Terry lived pretty close to school, and his parents were never there. There were a whole bunch of us at the house. We smoked pot on his balcony. I found a chain in Terry's room that went with some fake dog tags. Everyone went downstairs and made bologna sandwiches with white bread and yellow mustard. I didn't eat mine.

While everyone was eating, I took the dog tags off the chain and cut little holes in the pig's ears with a kitchen knife, and then I put the chain through the holes. I had a pig-head necklace.

We stayed at Terry's for fifth period. Then Danny Camillo came over and sold me some acid. I got five tabs for twenty bucks. It was Felix the Cat brand. There were these little Felix the Cat heads on all the tabs. I didn't want to go back to school, so I went home. I hung the pig head from my rearview mirror.

I had my own apartment because my dad owned the building. My dad and mom were on the same floor as I was, and my little sister lived with them. My older brother also had his own apartment. I called my place the Punisher pad. I had a Punisher poster on the wall. It was a white skull, without a jaw, against a black background. I took one tab of acid, and I watched porn on my couch for an hour. Rex walked in, and I gave him a tab of acid. We had time, so we watched a movie, *Less Than Zero*. It was bad. Rex said that he read the book and it was better. I had to get up and get some water on my face. I went to the bathroom, and I couldn't find myself in the mirror. Then I found myself. I didn't look like Warren Beatty at all.

I peeked out the door to where Rex was sitting on the couch. He had his back to me, and he was doing big whooping laughs at the television.

I didn't come out of the bathroom for a long time. I sat on the toilet. I saw space and time.

I came out. Rex was lying down on the floor. He was watching *Full House*. I was still looking in the mirror even though it was in the other room.

"I'm not driving you out to Santa Cruz like this," I said. "We'll get Naps to drive."

We called Seth. He was at home. He said he wasn't supposed to go out because he got suspended. Rex told him to fuck off, and to drive us to Santa Cruz.

"I thought it was a private party."

"Well it was," I said. "But now it's not."

There was a silence on the other end. Then Seth said, "Okay, I'll be right over. I have to ride my bike."

Seth came over, and I was trying to keep him quiet because of my dad being in the next apartment even though he never really heard anything.

I didn't want Seth to know that we were on acid. You couldn't trust him when he was high. After a bit he said, "Are you guys high?" Rex and I were sitting right next to each other on the couch. Rex looked at me, but said nothing. It looked like there was a baby goldfish in his eye. I turned back to Seth and told him we were just high on weed. He asked for some, and I said it was all gone.

I didn't even want to go to Santa Cruz.

Seth drove us. I was in the front seat, and Rex was in the back. The little piglet head hung from the rearview. We drove on the 17, and it winds a lot and it goes up this mountain through all these woods before it dumps you out at the beach. It was dark, and I just watched all the dark trees go by. We listened to Dr. Dre and 2Pac and DJ Quik. When the bass hit hard I could see it. The trees shook to the bass. I closed my eyes, and there were white bass circles.

My dad and mom used to take me and my older brother and my younger sister out to Santa Cruz. We'd always go to a beach called Capitola. In my memories, it's beautiful. There were these different-colored adobe houses, right on the beach. We'd rent one out and stay for a week during the summer. There was this lake next to the beach, with a great big railroad bridge over it, and it was so high and big and black. I once saw this Western, and this guy had to jump off a bridge like that because he was on the run. He had an arrow in his chest, and he couldn't pull it out, so he broke it off and went around with the point stuck inside him for the whole film.

My family and I would take the 17 through the woods. About halfway up the mountain, there were these two large cat sculptures. They were guarding a gate in the trees. I would look for them every time we went. Even when I was older and was getting in a lot of trouble, I would still look for them.

We passed the cats in the dark. I saw them looming, white and large and hazy. I dreamed about the road, I must have been asleep for a bit, and then Seth and Rex were yelling at each other. Seth was freaking out. He saw I was awake, and he started clawing me.

"What the fuck is going on?" I said.

We kept yelling the question at each other as we wrestled. I checked my pockets.

"Where the fuck is my acid?" I said.

"I ate it all!" he yelled.

"He's fucking gone," said Rex from the backseat. While I was asleep, Rex had fallen asleep too. Seth had found my acid and had been driving around for two hours through the woods. "He's out of his mind."

Now Seth was blank, and dumb; his eyes were wide and the vein in his neck pumped fast and mechanically.

"What happened?" I said.

"I think we hit a deer," said Rex.

"Fuck you," I said. This road was beautiful. I knew that, even if I couldn't see it through the dark. Seth didn't say anything. He just looked straight ahead and drove. All the intensity of the yelling was now submerged into the heavy atmosphere of non-talking. The only sound was a whirring sound, like something was dragging at the front of the car. I opened the door, and the thick whirring got louder. Then the whirring stopped, and it was just the rushing sound of air. I shut the door.

"I think we're okay," I said. Nobody answered me.

I had Seth pull the car over. There was something stuck to the front of the grille, but I didn't look too closely. We got in, Rex climbed into the front, and I drove the rest of the way. The pig head dangled from the rearview. He had his little burned-out eyes and his little tongue sticking out. Rex grabbed him and threw him out the window.

We passed the two big cat statues again. On our left this time.

I got us down to the 101 and then north to Palo Alto. I knew exactly where I was going. There's a public parking structure across from my father's building. I parked on the top level. Rex and I got out, and Seth got out of the back, and we went to the front of the car. The car was under a tall light. In the grille, there was a hoof. It had bent the metal. There was a big part of the leg left, all the way past the knee.

I took the skinny part in my hands, the bloody part under my armpit, and I yanked the hoof out of the metal. I threw the leg over the side of the parking structure.

MEN
boys

I put this photo
in the yearbook +
Marshal Kooh scratched
out "MEN" and wrote "boys."

Yosemite

The drive up to Yosemite was long. My father played Bach the whole first half. We drove through Milpitas, Pleasanton, Dublin, Manteca, Escalon, and Oakdale. We had been to Yosemite before with my mom, but that was when it was snowing. There wasn't going to be snow this time, and it was just me and my dad and my brother.

At the turnoff for the Old Yosemite Road, the sun turned tangerine and my dad took out the Bach and put in a tape of his meditation lady. My brother and I chanted with her using funny voices, but that only lasted a few minutes, then we were quiet again. My dad drove and hummed quietly to himself. My brother and I would trade the front seat at every rest stop. I was two years older, but I got carsick more easily, so I got the front longer. I had been in the front since East Oakdale. The Old Yosemite Road was crooked, and my dad drove slower. Soon the sky was getting gray, but there was purple above the mountains. My brother was asleep in the back. He was slanted over with his face in all the puffy jackets.

"Dad, can I turn the heat up?"

"Yup."

I did and cupped my hand over the grate until it was too hot and I pulled it away. I wasn't tired even though it was dark outside and we'd been driving for hours. I leaned forward but my seat belt held me, so I undid it and leaned again and picked up my father's old thick Bible with loose pages sticking out and a rubber band around it.

"Put your belt back on," he said.

"I know," I said. I clicked it in place. "I was just picking this up."

"My Bible."

"I know," I said. "Why are the lines colored?"

There was yellow, pink, and green highlighter, all faded, all over the pages.

"Those are passages I like."

I asked him why.

"Because they help me."

I read a little. *Surely goodness and mercy shall follow me all the days of my life.* It meant nothing. I closed it. "You go to church?"

"No," he said. The lady and the people on the meditation tape were chanting softly.

"Why do you have the Bible?"

"I just open it when I get in the car. Whatever page it opens to, I read."

"Why?"

"I told you, it helps me."

I put the rubber band back around the leather cover and held the thick thing on my lap. We went through a town with only a few lights, and my dad slowed. The headlights bounced off some signs into my eyes. One said YOSEMITE 30 MILES. Then we were on the winding part going up the mountain. The tape came to the end, and my dad ejected it and left it sticking out of the player. It was white. The Bible tried to slip down my leg, and I held on to it.

"Adam and Eve," I said.

"Yup," my dad said.

"Noah."

"Yup."

"Moses, Abraham. Jesus, David. The flood, killing the ram, the plagues, first there was light, then darkness, then water, then land, then the garden of Eden."

"Where did you learn all that?"

"At Sunday school, where Mom takes us."

"Unity?"

"Yeah."

We got quiet as we wound up the mountain. The car went so close to the sides, and there wasn't always a barrier. Last time we did this part of the drive in the dark too and I hated it. I secretly held on to the side of the door with my right hand. There were pennies in the handle, and I pushed them back and forth in the holder with my index finger. Dad's AA medallion was in there too.

I hoisted up a little and tried to look over the side of the cliff, but there were just trees and black, and there was too much back and forth, so I sat back. I tried to pretend we were going into the Misty Mountains and there were goblins around us, but I felt dizzy and I stopped. We kept going, and I couldn't sleep; all I could do was sit there.

"You want to know what my dad did with me when I was little?"

"What?" We were talking quietly because of my brother in the back.

"Nothing." He laughed a little. "My dad was a son of a bitch."

We were quiet for a while.

"Why do we go to Yosemite all the time?"

"We've only been a couple times. You don't like it?"

"No, I do. I like the Ahwahnee. But why do we go?"

"I guess because nature makes me feel good. And I want to spend time with you and Alex."

"Because you love us?"

"Yeah, because I love you, and I've missed you."

At the Ahwahnee there was no one around. We parked and followed the footlights along the stone path. My dad carried Alex in one arm and his suitcase in his other hand. I followed with my heavy backpack. The lady at the desk gave my dad a card key, and I followed his footsteps down the red carpet with the boxy Indian designs.

In the room, my dad laid Alex on one of the two beds and told me to get into my pajamas. He got some things from his suitcase and went into the bathroom, then the water started running. I took off my shoes and socks and jeans and put on my gray sweatpants and took my toothbrush into the bathroom. I was barefoot, and the floor was cold. My dad was in his T-shirt, sitting on the toilet in the corner.

"You should knock."

"Sorry, I heard water."

"It's okay. Brush your teeth." I just stood there and looked only at myself in the mirror.

"There's some toothpaste in my toiletry bag there." The square black bag unzipped around the whole side and opened like a mouth. There were two gray Bic razors, and a blue-and-red can of shaving cream that said BARBASOL, and a small white-and-green tube of toothpaste with a Roman column on it. The toothpaste was grainy on my brush and chalky in my mouth. If I looked at the border of the mirror I could see a slanted version of my dad wiping. He stayed on the seat and put the toilet paper between his legs. I always stood up to do it. He wiped for a long time, and I mostly looked in my own eyes. Then he was behind me.

"If you brush like that you're going to ruin your gums."

"No I'm not."

"Do it like this." He took his brush and did strokes in only one direction at a time. Starting from the gums, he went down on the top teeth and then up on the bottom teeth. My dad's teeth were long and

120

nice, except one in the front was yellow. He also had heavy eyelids that made him look a little evil.

We went to bed. I lay in the bed with Alex, but he didn't wake up. My eyes got used to the dark, and I wandered them down the red band of Indian patterns at the top of the wall. The design was like one long zigzagging tunnel. The room was dark and quiet and full of bodies, and I fell asleep.

In the morning we ate in the great hall. The walls were made of stone, and there was a fire in the large stone fireplace in the center. The pillars around the room were huge, made out of real trees.

"Pancakes are good for hiking," my father said. "Try to eat all of them."

I tried. I had pancakes and orange juice and hot chocolate, and Alex had French toast and hot chocolate, and my father ate scrambled eggs and bacon and black coffee. It was all stuff that we didn't usually eat; we usually had cereal at home. There were also little circular plastic jelly containers with pictures of fruit on them, dewy orange slices, a huge glistening strawberry, two raspberries, side by side, plump and wet. I didn't have any toast because of the pancakes, but I lined the jellies up at the top of my plate. Five colorful circles.

"Alex only ate some of his French toast," I said. Three halves of the toast were still there soaked in a swamp of syrup.

"He's smaller."

"Why do I have to eat all my pancakes?"

"You don't. But they're good for energy. That's what hikers do: they eat a bunch of carbohydrates, and your body keeps them inside as spare energy when you need it. If we're going to go to Yosemite Falls, then you'll need your energy."

"Can we go down the waterfall?" said Alex.

"No, stupid, you'd die," I said.

"Don't say that." For a second he was frozen in my direction; I could smell him, the rich Barbasol. His eyes released me and turned to my brother. "Yes, you would die. The waterfall is very powerful, and there are rocks at the bottom. But every once in a while someone gets trapped in the current at the top and they go over by accident."

"And they die?" said Alex.

"Yup."

"I don't want to die," said Alex.

"Everyone dies," I said.

"I'm not going to."

"You have to," I said. "You're going to freakin' die."

"Chris, stop." My dad didn't get loud, but he took my hand and squeezed. "Alex," he said to my brother. "You might have to die, but it will be okay."

Alex shook his head.

"Dying isn't bad; it's just another trip. Like our trip here, to Yosemite. It's like going to another Yosemite."

Alex said, "I hate Yosemite, and I hate dying."

My dad was done with his eggs and had only half a piece of bacon left neatly at the side of his plate. He had put his knife and fork in the center to signal that he was finished. I put my knife and fork the same way on top of the last downy pancake.

My dad sipped his coffee then put the mug down and said, "I know you boys don't like coming to Yosemite. But I think when you're older you'll appreciate it. I never had a place like this when I was young. And if you really don't like it, we never need to come again. Okay?"

"I want to never come again," said Alex.

"I like Yosemite," I said.

"You can go on the waterfall and die," said Alex.

"Shut up," I said. I mashed one of his French toasts with my thumb. Alex whined, and it looked like he was going to cry.

"Alex, stop. Chris, stop." We both sat still. "Listen. Neither of you is going to die for a very long time. I promise. And when you do, you can go anywhere you want. It doesn't have to be Yosemite. It can be any place."

"Round Table," said Alex. He meant Round Table Pizza.

On the trail we walked in a line. I was last. We had our puffy jackets on, but it wasn't too cold. Mine was brown and lighter brown, Alex's was red and blue, and my dad's was all blue, bigger and less puffy. I told myself brown was better than red and blue.

The sun was low and shot shafts of gold at an angle through the trees. From far away I could see insects and atmosphere dancing, but when I walked through the light it was warm and the insects were gone. The ground was dry. No one was around. It was just us walking.

Our first stop was supposed to be a bunch of caves. My dad pointed up off the trail, and we walked up an incline. After a bit, as we walked up the hill, I could see some people standing in front of the caves. When we got closer, I saw that they were a man and a woman in their thirties, wearing shorts and hiking boots and back-packs. The man had light curly hair like mine, but his was down to his ears, and the woman had long straight brown hair. Her legs were thin like a horse's, and on her knee there was a purple-brown scab.

"How's it going?" my dad said.

"Not bad," the man said. "Some candles here." We walked up closer and saw that there was a large circle of white candles in the dirt. The circle was large enough for a person to lie in the middle.

"There's another one in there," the man said, and pointed up toward the cave. My father said nothing, but he took Alex's hand.

Not long before, I had gone to see *The Little Mermaid* with my Mom and Alex at the Old Mill Theater. Seeing movies was one of our traditions. In the middle of the movie I got up and went to the bathroom. On the way back I looked into another theater playing a movie called *The First Power.* Lou Diamond Phillips was in it. I knew that it was about the devil and I wasn't supposed to watch, but I loved him as Chavez in *Young Guns,* so I stayed for a few minutes. The killer had tied up a woman and put her in the middle of a circle of candles. She was gagged and scared. The killer told her to relax and said he was going to say his prayers backward: "Heaven in art which father our . . ." I left and went back to *The Little Mermaid*, but I couldn't forget what I saw.

My father didn't let us look at the candles in the cave, so we kept walking. He held Alex's hand, and I walked a little behind them. My father and brother both had straight brown hair. The sun was above us, and it was hotter. My dad took off his jacket, and I took off mine. Alex took his off, and we stopped to wait for him to tie it around his waist, but he couldn't do it, so my dad carried it for him.

The next stop was El Capitan.

It was a tall boxy mountain that shot straight up out of the ground. In my mind I always thought of it as yellow-orange because I thought of all the mountains in colors: Half Dome was white and gray; Mount Lyell was green; Mount Dana was pink; Matterhorn

Peak was blue; but up close El Capitan wasn't yellow-orange, it was just dirty-white and chalky.

"Look at that tree," my dad said. It was a tree with reddish bark. High up some of the branches had been ripped away, and in places the bark was skinned off, revealing the pale insides.

"That's fresh. It's from rocks falling off the mountain."

There was a little stream going almost next to the base of the mountain. I told my dad I didn't want any rocks to fall on me, and he promised that they wouldn't. Then he gave us time to explore on our own. I had nothing to do, so I found a place with some sun and I sat with my back against the mountain. I took my shoes off and let my feet feel the air. The water was very close, and it trickled and sparkled. From somewhere close I could hear my brother's voice, high and demanding, and my father's voice, deep and calming.

Sitting in the sun I felt empty. I was a black center in the middle of all the nature. I was nothing, but I could do anything. I could fill myself with anything. I said a prayer. I asked God that I would never be like my father. I told God that I didn't want to have sons. I said that if I died, I would like to have done something good before that happened. I prayed that my brother would die, and then I took it back.

Later, on a large flat oval rock, we had our lunch. The hotel had packed us sandwiches and Cokes. I had turkey on wheat with sprouts and cranberries. It was the best sandwich I'd ever eaten. The Coke washed it down, and the sugary syrup stuck to my teeth.

To get to Yosemite Falls we walked through a very green and wet part of the park. The ground was full of mud and damp needles. All the rocks were wet and had a blue gloss. Soon the noise of the falls started growing, and after a while the sound was all around us.

A steady rush of horror saying, "You are small and insignificant," and getting so loud that you just wanted to see to get it over with and get out of there. Some people were walking back from the falls toward us. A couple with dark hair and dark clothes. They said nothing as they passed.

The three of us, we three Petersons, walked in a line toward the noise, my father in the center. We had our puffy jackets back on, and there was a mist around us. The mist wet our faces as we continued toward the center of the roar. It felt like something was pushing us back, but my father kept pulling us forward. The trees were green and black over us, like the arched ceiling of a church.

Then we came out from under the trees and there was a huge rock face and in the center, a cataract, white and gushing, implacable and steady in its furious rush over the side. It was a violent slice of movement in the stolid graphite-colored rock front, and the scene was all glazed over by the shifting atmosphere of mist. The waterfall was farther than I imagined, but the sound roared in a chorus that echoed and reechoed without end. It felt like there were loudspeakers just below us projecting the rushing noise, so loud and close when the waterfall was so far.

We stood for a minute and then made our way up the damp path to a wooden bridge that spanned the river. At the base of the bridge, the waterfall sent itself smashing on the rocks. It was even louder here, as if we were in a cave of sound. The waterfall was a mystery. It was water and rock and river and time and noise. *Is the water the waterfall?* I wondered. *Or the rock formation that makes the waterfall in that way? Or the combination?* You could take a photo, but the water captured in the picture would never flow over the waterfall again.

An old man walked over the bridge. He had on a translucent blue raincoat with the hood up and pulled tight around his face so that only his eyes and nose were showing through the opening. We asked him to take a picture of us, and he did, with our backs to the railing of the bridge and the waterfall behind us. Alex was in my father's arms.

The way back felt too far. I knew my father had kept us out too long. We had to walk back past El Capitan. The sun was going down behind the tall square mountain and there was an orange glow bending around one edge. My dad had my brother on his shoulders, and I was dragging my feet. After a while, we left the footpath and walked along a larger dirt road. My father said we were almost back to the hotel, but he had been saying that for a long time. A little off the road there were the remains of the wall of an old stone house. Next to the wall was the wasted foundation. Behind this was another foundation with brick remains ringing its sides. The sun was almost gone.

We walked for what seemed like an hour; the sun was gone, and the sky was purple. I didn't want to go any farther. Yosemite was hell. Then ahead we saw some burning. As we got closer we saw that there were large burning piles of leaves just off the road. I walked ahead of my father and brother to look at the piles. They were on a stretch of dirt so that the fire wouldn't spread, but the flames went really high. There were five piles about twenty-five feet wide, all taller than I was, and the flames leaped taller than my dad. Many of the leaves and branches and sticks had thorns on them, and I thought that they might have been poison ivy or poison oak. The smell was thick in my throat. When I was across from the second burning pile I saw something large and white through the smoke, very close to the pile. I walked to the edge of the road and saw that it was a human rib cage. I didn't see a head, but the ribs were very clear, like a corset. I ran back.

"Dad, there's a skeleton over there." My dad put my brother on the ground and told us to wait. He walked to the piles and stood over where the skeleton was. He stood there for a while and then came back to us and put my brother back on his shoulders. "Let's go. A mountain climber must have fallen off the mountain. The animals got to him. It's okay, come on, let's go." We quickly walked past the piles. "Don't look," my dad said, but I did. The pointed ends of the white ribs in the orange light of the fire.

My father started humming the meditation songs. My brother cried quietly, and my father bounced him gently and said it was okay, it was just a hiker that had an accident. He hummed again, and I walked by his side and held his hand. The fire was far behind us, but it still felt close. My footsteps crunched, and I didn't want to be on the ground. It was hard to see, and for ten minutes in the dark he hummed to us.

Then we were back at the hotel. We took our jackets off, and my dad said, "We're stinky-boys. We're all going to take showers. Then we'll order room service, okay? Who's first shower?"

Nobody spoke. My brother and I sat on the bed.

Alex said, "Can we call Mom?"

"No, it's too late to bother Mom."

I said, "Dad, call the police."

My dad picked up the phone.

"Can I have the ranger service please? Thanks . . ." He waited a bit, and we watched. "Hello, I was out walking with my boys near

El Capitan, and we came across some burning piles. Next to the piles there was a skeleton, I think it must have been a climber that fell off the mountain . . . No, the animals got to him . . . Yeah, they even went through the sheathing on the bones . . . No, no head. No arms either. But there were feet . . . Yes, they looked human to me . . . sure . . ." Then he waited with the phone to his ear. I was glad we were together because it felt like the world outside was full of murder.

Then he was talking again. "I see . . . Oh, really. Um, hmmm . . . interesting, okay, thank you very much. Yes, the Ahwahnee, room 213, Peterson. Yes, okay, thank you very much." He hung up the phone. "It sounds like it was a bear."

"I saw, it was human," I said. "It was real, I saw."

"I know, but the rangers said it was a bear. It was getting too friendly with the people because people were feeding it, so they had to shoot it."

"It was a bear," Alex said.

"Shut up, you didn't even look," I said.

"Don't worry, Chris, I thought it was a person too."

"But why would they shoot the bear if it was being friendly?"

"Because a bear's idea of friendly is different than ours. Bears just want food, so they'll kill you if you have it."

My brother took the first shower and then my dad. He came out with a towel around his waist. He was pale and thin. Before I went in I told my dad I wanted a cheeseburger for dinner. The water couldn't get warm enough. I lathered the soap in my hands and rubbed it under my pits and around my neck and then down across my chest and ribs and crotch. Then I did my legs and feet and then my crack. When I was lathering my face the water got cold, so I danced in place while I washed off the soap. I didn't wash my hair.

After I dried off in the bathroom I put on my gray sweatpants and a red T-shirt that had the AA circle and triangle on it from one of the picnics and went into the main room. The food was there, and we sat on the two beds and ate from the table on wheels. We all had burgers and Cokes. The buns were toasted, and the cheese was salty and good. The burger was so thick I could hardly fit the first bites in my mouth, and the tomatoes and onions squeezed out the back. My brother had a regular hamburger. He put tons of ketchup on all his hamburgers; I used mustard only because I was more mature. My dad put mustard on his, but spicy mustard made with white wine. He said all the alcohol was cooked out so it was okay for him to eat it.

After dinner my dad put the table outside the door. While he was out my brother and I started jumping on the beds, then we started jumping over the gap between the beds.

"Hey guys, settle down, settle down, I want to tell you something." We stopped jumping, and I sat on the edge, and Alex lay on his stomach. My dad sat on the edge of his bed where he had sat while he was eating.

"Do you guys know how babies are made?"

"I think so," I said.

"How?"

"The husband and wife get naked in a bath together."

"Sick," said Alex.

"Who told you that?" my dad said to me.

"Beatrice." Beatrice was my best friend, a French girl that lived down the street. We had had chicken pox at the same time, and watched *The Dukes of Hazzard* together, and the movie *Time Bandits*. She had itched her chicken pox and got an indent between her eyes, like she'd been hit by a miniature cork.

"Beatrice is wrong," said my dad. "Yes, the man and the woman get naked, but they don't have to get into the bath. Usually they do it in a bed."

"Why?"

"Because it's comfortable there."

"Why are they naked?" said my brother.

"Because the man needs to put his penis in the woman's vagina."

"*What?*" I said. My brother was squealing and squirming on the bed beside me.

"When two people are in love, that's what they do. It's not gross if you love each other . . ."

"You and Mom?" I said.

"Yes."

My brother was really going crazy with the squeals then, rolling onto the floor. My dad and I started laughing.

"You did that for me and Alex?" I said.

My dad nodded. "Yes."

"That is gross," I said, and my brother repeated, "Gross!"

Then I asked, "Do you still do it?"

My dad took a long time. He was frozen, his eyelids were heavy, and his eyes looked low. Finally he turned his face up to mine and smiled. His yellow tooth was showing, and he did a quiet laugh, exhaling twice.

Then we all got ready for bed. I let my dad and my brother brush their teeth first, and then I went in there alone. I tried to brush the way my dad had told me to, but it didn't feel right, so I just brushed my old way. The bear had ribs like I had ribs. Underneath had been lungs, and a stomach and a heart, and they all got burned away.

Senior boys Calendar,
all the studs. Sort of.

Friend of the Devil

He drove into the high school lot and parked behind the baseball diamond. The lot was full of cars, but there was no one around. He turned the key, and the engine stopped.

It was his grandfather's car. A 1990 Nissan Stanza with Ohio plates. His grandmother gave him the car because his grandfather was dead.

Whenever Teddy reached for something that he'd dropped under the seat, his hand would be covered in his grandfather's white hair.

It was Teddy's second car. The first was a rusty blue 1973 VW Bug. He worked for two years at the golf course in order to get the VW. He drove the little caged cart that picked up the balls on the driving range. Teddy would hold his books below the steering wheel and read while he picked up the balls. He loved Kerouac's *On the Road* and Faulkner's *The Sound and the Fury.*

The VW was a piece of shit. It had no parking brake and no stereo, and the driver's side window had to be propped up by a wedge of cardboard or it would drop down into the door. In the corner of the cardboard he had written in tiny script *Fuck you god.*

Teddy used to drive the VW around town and sing to himself because he didn't have a stereo. He sang Bob Dylan and The Doors. Sometimes he drove drunk.

One morning he pulled into the school parking lot and the brake pedal dropped to the floor. The parking brake was broken too. Out loud he said, "Fuck, shit, fuck."

He circled around the parking lot, hoping to slow down. No one knew his car was out of control. Everyone just walked around like any other time.

Then he came to the end of the parking lot.

He popped up over the curb and onto the grass. The people knew something was happening then. There was a shout. He passed two guys in baseball caps, and their heads swiveled slow as he went past; they were laughing.

He rolled into the middle of the quad at five miles an hour. People were up and running to look. He thought about diving from the car, but he didn't.

Then he had a choice between running the car into the science building or hitting the lone sycamore tree in the center of the quad.

He steered the car at the tree and waited for impact. It hit, and he jerked forward. The seat belt cut a smile into the side of his neck.

He unhooked the seat belt and got out. The center of the hood was pushed in. The wrinkles around the dent made it look like a brain.

Everyone walked over and stood around. Someone started whooping. Everyone laughed and whooped and clapped like it was a joke. Then a teacher came out. Mrs. Benny, the chemistry teacher. She was black. She had short hair and a big ass. When she saw no one was hurt, she started yelling. She cursed at him. She called him a "fucking idiot." She thought he was drunk.

He wasn't drunk that time. He just had bad luck.

Fuck you god.

Now he had his grandfather's car. But his grandfather was dead.

Teddy was seventeen, and he was on probation. That was because of the other arrests.

He didn't want to go to class. He sat in his grandfather's Nissan and did nothing. He just looked out. The bleachers and the wooden backstop were hunter green. They were comforting. He had played baseball here when he was a kid. He had never been good. When he was twelve he had to play in the pitching machine league when all the good players were in the real pitching league.

He looked intently at the deep green of the worn boards of the backstop, and they were a reminder of his inadequacy. It was sad and pleasing to think about his failure at sports. He liked to think he wasn't like the athletes. And he wasn't.

First period had started thirty minutes ago. He leaned forward and pulled out a 1.75-liter bottle of gin from underneath the seat. It was half finished and sloshed in the bottle. The bottle had his grandfather's white soft hair on it.

His grandfather had been an oral surgeon. He didn't go to medical school because he hated math. This was a strange excuse. Teddy hated math too.

His grandfather changed his name from Weinstein to West back in the '50s. His mother's maiden name was Carol West. It didn't sound Jewish at all. Once, in Ohio, when he was little, Teddy looked through a copy of his grandfather's Edgar Allan Poe stories. In the front it said DANIEL WEINSTEIN. Teddy showed his grandfather, and his grandfather scribbled it out.

Now he was dead. There were over two hundred people at his funeral. His name was Dan, and someone read some lyrics from "Danny Boy": "Oh, Danny boy, the pipes, the pipes are calling." Teddy cried then.

His grandfather, when he was alive, told him to read Dostoyevsky, Tolstoy, and Melville.

Beefeater. It was hot and bit the back of his throat, and the feeling stayed there. He drank again, lifting the bottle toward the ceiling in a quick jerk. He squeezed it through the tight gap at the back of his throat. It went down into his empty stomach. He thought of the old guys. Faulkner with his pipe and Hem with his bulls. Drinkers.

There had been three arrests. Stealing at Macy's, cologne. Graffiti in the park. And a fight with a knife. He had been drunk, on a front lawn. A football player came at him. Teddy had a knife he always kept. Stuck it in the guy's arm. In his bicep. It stuck there, and blood poured out, more blood than an arm could possibly hold. After that Teddy was on probation.

One more arrest and it was jail, they said.

The stealing was when he was thirteen. He didn't need the cologne, he already had fifteen bottles; it was just something to do. They would slip the sample bottles into their pants. The last time they were spotted, and on their way out a big male clerk caught him and held him. His friends got away. He waited with the clerk and the store manager until the police came.

The officers arrived. A middle-aged Latino with a large mustache and a white guy with carrot-colored hair. The Latino talked to Teddy in the manager's office. He told him he might go to juvenile hall. Teddy cried.

Then they left. They walked Teddy out in handcuffs even though he was just a boy. Teddy sat in the hard plastic backseat of the police cruiser, while the officers talked casually.

"Prince said he got there and she was already dead."

"Have you seen *Batman Returns* yet?"

"Yeah, with my kid, good movie."

It seemed like they had forgotten about Teddy. The rest of the car ride was silent.

The officers took him to the station. They put him in the interrogation room and left. It was a brown closet-sized room with a table and a chair. There was nothing to think about. Just blackness in his head.

Then the Latino policeman came in and gave him a Xerox copy of an article about juvenile hall. It was dated 1987, back when Teddy was nine. It was about the bad conditions in juvenile hall. It talked about a kid getting stabbed seventeen times by a pencil. The police wanted the article to scare him. It was a routine.

In the end he just had to do some community service. Two months after the arrest, he and some other kids walked around University Avenue and picked up trash. It was a sunny day and pretty fun.

If only he were good at baseball, maybe that would have changed his life. Or football or soccer or basketball. He never was. His dad tried to teach him, but somehow it wasn't enough. The other kids were better.

His dad was an alcoholic. His dad went to AA. Every Saturday until Teddy was ten, his dad would take him to a meeting.

The meeting was in a large church auditorium with a red-and-white checked floor. The tiles were slanted so they looked like diamonds and not squares. The bathrooms had huge white porcelain urinals. The auditorium smelled like coffee. Teddy would eat the cookies that were next to the large tin coffee casks in the back. When there were no cookies, he would suck on the sugar cubes.

Outside, in front of the church, there were old coffee cans where people put their cigarettes. That was where everyone smoked. Usually the men and women that smoked had tattoos.

When he was a kid he liked the yellow camel on the cigarette box. One time a guy with dragons all over his arms showed Teddy the secret picture on the camel box. It was a picture of a girl giving a blowjob. That was the first time he heard *blowjob*.

He smoked now. Marlboro reds. He pulled one out and lit it and cracked the window. There were secret pictures on the Marlboro box too. Three *K*s. That meant that the Marlboro man was in the KKK. He knew that was stupid, but maybe it was true, in some place, somewhere.

His father hadn't cared about the little arrests, the stealing or the graffiti, but he had gotten mad about the knife in the arm. More because of the drinking. Teddy wasn't supposed to drink because of his dad's problem. After he stabbed the kid with the knife, his dad made Teddy go to AA himself.

Everyone in the meetings was much older. He recognized the same people from when he used to go as a kid.

He would go in the nighttime after school. He met a Vietnam veteran named Mack.

Mack had a face that was shattered. He had deep scars below his eyes, and the skin around his cheeks and jaw drooped like a Saint Bernard's. He was skinny and tall and spoke deep and slow. His hair was short and orange. He smoked American Spirits and drank venti lattes from Starbucks.

They would hang out together, Teddy and Mack. They'd go to night meetings then over to Starbucks on University. They would sit outside and smoke. Mack would have a latte with lots of sweetener. Teddy had a grande coffee, black.

Sometimes a retarded guy named Andy would come along. He wasn't fully retarded, but he was off. When he was talking normal it seemed like he was yelling. He liked to have as many friends as he could, like a little kid. He couldn't drive. He would ride around town on his mountain bike, going from meeting to meeting. Andy was at every meeting. He had nothing better to do. He always wore a dark orange bike helmet with a Grateful Dead sticker on it. Sometimes he forgot to take his helmet off. Even when he was standing outside Starbucks talking.

Teddy would say, "I hate not drinking because I want to be like Hemingway."

"That's a silly way to think," said Mack.

"Why?"

"What do you like about Hemingway?"

"I don't know. He was charismatic. And he did a lot of things. It seems like drinking had a lot to do with whatever he did."

"Like shooting himself?"

"I guess. But still."

Then they started going to the VA together. Mack could take them because he was a veteran. They would go to an AA meeting and then go over to the VA and play pool. Teddy was terrible at pool, but it seemed like it was something he should get good at. The guys in movies were all good at it. So was Neal Cassady.

It was the VA where Kesey worked when he wrote *Cuckoo's Nest*. Teddy and Mack would play pool at night, and there would be a few guys hanging around watching TV. Usually there was an old movie on, like *Jailhouse Rock* or *Cool Hand Luke*.

This was all before.

The parking lot was heating up. He took a sip of warm gin and looked at the sand around the diamond.

The Devil got in the car with him and sat shotgun. The Devil lit up a cigarette, and he and Teddy both sat in his grandfather's car and smoked.

"I guess you didn't stay sober."

"No."

"Hope your dad doesn't find out."

"Fuck him. He had his time to drink. I'm only seventeen. I should get my time."

"You already got in a lot of trouble. Don't you think it's a bad idea?"

"Everyone my age drinks."

"Not everyone. And certainly not in the parking lot before school."

He and the Devil sat there and smoked. The Devil had a drink of gin. The clear liquid went down and sat in his red devil belly.

When he was at the VA Mack used to talk to Teddy. Mack was older than him by thirty years, but he didn't have anyone else to talk to, so he talked to Teddy. They would play pool and talk. Mack said, "My girl is gonna break up with me."

"Why?"

"Because I caught her cheating on me with this other guy."

Andy was sitting on one of the old couches, watching *Mad Max Beyond Thunderdome* on the hanging TV. He couldn't hear them.

"So why don't you dump *her*."

"Because I love her."

"Who did she cheat with?"

"That fucker Manuel that goes to Hamilton on Sundays."

"I hate that meeting."

"Me too."

The Devil was looking out at the baseball field. It was empty, and the parking lot was empty. It was only nine in the morning, but the rising sun was blasting through the windshield. The heat accumulated in the car. It went in and didn't go out. Teddy sat there and smoked and sweated.

"You don't talk to Mack anymore," said the Devil.

"No. He's dead."

"What about retarded Andy?"

"Sometimes I see him riding around on his bike with his stupid Grateful Dead helmet."

"I hate the Grateful Dead."

"I like them." He looked at the Devil. "Friend of the Devil is a friend of mine."

"Nice."

They each had another sip of gin. It was so hot in the car now. Even the Devil was sweating in the sun. They each lit another cigarette and smoked in the car. The windows were cracked just enough for them to ash through. Some ash fell back inside and burned the seat. It gave off a nasty plastic smell.

Mack told Teddy about Nam only once.

"There was this kid. We were going into this village, and some people started shooting at us. We shot back, and I shot this kid in the bushes. After the shooting stopped, we went over and his body was there. We pulled his pants off, and this kid had the biggest schlong I'd ever seen. Like a snake. They got a picture of me kneeling next to him holding that thing. I was grinning, giving a thumbs-up."

They stood there at the pool table not saying anything. Teddy didn't take his shot.

"I know I'm going to hell for that."

"We're all going to hell," said the Devil.

"Shut up."

"I think so."

"I don't believe you."

When the Devil inhaled, the cigarette crackled. His skin on his cheeks was as red as the red of the Marlboro box.

There was a lone girl crossing the parking lot. She was too far away to recognize. The Devil watched her.

Teddy thought of girls. He thought of their vaginas and mouths and tits. He thought of blowjobs and circle jerks and assholes and cum. He thought of dicks going everywhere, in every orifice, and hot smelly balls, and people on their knees, and pubic hair, and drunk girls, and cum on faces, and swallowing, and sitting on toilets, and naked bodies, and saliva. His dad's hairy dick, and dicks he'd seen in the locker room, and girls in *Playboy*, and his calculus teacher's ass shaking when she wrote on the chalkboard. And Erin who gave blowjobs in the art building bathroom, and the first porno he ever watched—it had a haunted-house theme, and they all wandered around the haunted mansion and had sex.

And then he thought of bubbly carbuncles all over everything. They were white and pus-filled and were all over every dick and pussy and mouth. They were everywhere.

He looked away from the Devil and out the windshield. There were no clouds. The sun burned a hole in the sky. The sun was in the car.

One time he asked Mack about war in general.

"What do you think about war in general?"

"It's shit."

"Yeah."

"It's hell and worth nothing."

"What about World War II? That saved the Jews, right?"

"Yeah. But that was their problem."

"What do you mean?"

"I think the Jews let that whole thing happen to them."

There was nothing left to ask.

Soon after, Mack went to the hospital for cancer. Teddy meant to visit, but it all happened so quickly and then Mack died.

The bell for second period rang, and the Devil disappeared.

Teddy drank from the gin bottle again. There was only a third left. He would have to get more soon.

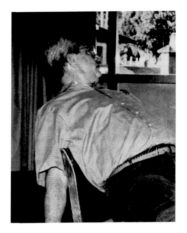

Mr. B.

Memoria

My dad lives in Russia. I haven't seen him in a few years. Ten years. He sent me a jacket from the Russian army last Christmas. He took all the army patches off. I wear it all the time. There are two or three things that people always talk about with me: my pale skin and my white hair and my jacket. I got all those from my dad.

It was the day of the homecoming dance. That morning I went to get a ride from Byron. He lives near me. He lives with his grandmother. Byron stays in the guesthouse behind the house. Everyone calls it "Guesthouse." When I got there, Byron's green Porsche wasn't out front, so I had to walk to school.

I took the long way, down California Ave. where the stores and restaurants are. At the end, just before the train tracks, there's a market called Mollie Stone's. I went in. I walked past the vegetable aisles to the chip rack. I wanted some Fritos. I was the only customer, and there was only one lady at the checkout counter. She was pretending not to look at me. But she was looking at me from the side of her face, like a fish. When a bus drove by she looked away and I stuffed some chips under my dad's jacket. I held them under my arm next to my heart.

I walked out, and the lady watched me. She had skin like crinkled paint on an old car.

I went to the end of California to the train tracks. There were morning commuters waiting for a train. I walked past them and down the tracks. It's like a secret pathway. No one is ever there, except bums sometimes.

I took out the chips; they were Ruffles potato chips, not Fritos. I didn't like Ruffles. A train passed. It was loud and huge. It was headed from San Francisco to San Jose.

In my jacket pocket, there was an Altoids tin that had two joints and a miniature red Bic lighter. I stole the joints from Harry, my stepdad.

I lit one. It was strong. It tasted like sweet tree bark. I put the tin back in the inside pocket of my jacket. After I smoked Harry's joint, I opened the bag of Ruffles and ate them. They tasted lemony.

I got to the place where the tracks met Churchill Ave. and walked across to school. I had physics. Inertia and kinetic energy. Mr. Moore was my teacher. He was young, and the girls said he was handsome. Sometimes he would play this character named Captain Physics. He would put on an old leather World War I aviator's hat and do a funny voice; he was a crazy science guy. It was supposed to make physics more interesting, but it didn't.

He was doing Captain Physics when I walked in and sat in my seat. I was enjoying the show a little because of the joint. It felt like bad TV. Like *Sesame Street*. The straps on his leather helmet were flapping, and his head looked like the tip of a brown penis.

Natasha Illichev was in my class. She was new to the school. She was from Russia, like me, but she sounded Russian. She was laughing at Captain Physics. Even her laugh sounded Russian.

After the Captain Physics show, Mr. Moore said something about my being late.

In creative writing class, Mr. Shotts read student stories that had been turned in the week before. They were all about a page long. He stood behind a little podium and read them aloud to the class, one after the other. He didn't tell who wrote which.

There was a story about a person's last minutes of life; he was on a plane that was about to crash. It was about a man, but I could tell a girl wrote it. At first the man was freaking out, but then he decided to read his book because there was nothing else to do. He was reading *The Brothers Karamazov*, and then he died.

There was this one about a guy and a girl having sex in a car at Foothills Park. I know it was Rahma's. Basically, they had sex and then the guy never called her again, and the girl was upset. In real life people called Rahma "Corn-the-Rahm" or "Rahma-mama," because Pete Eubanks stuck his thumb up her butt in a hot tub.

There was a really badly written story about a kid whose cousin was shot in East Palo Alto. It was Ezra's. He was the only one from East Palo Alto in the class.

Shotts read mine. It was about this guy who was in love with this blond girl. The girl was so pretty, she was like a doll. Every boy was in love with her. She thought she was fat, but she wasn't. She couldn't see how beautiful she was. The boy in the story had a burned face. His father had been in Vietnam. He kept all these old grenades from his war days in the garage. They were in a box with dust all over it, and no one touched them, but the boy knew where they were. One of them went off when the boy was playing with them, and it burned his face off.

The boy was in love with the blond girl. He would write poems to her, and one of the poems was in the story:

You're beautiful.
If I think about how beautiful you are,
It hurts.
When it hurts, I want to die.
I know I'm ugly, but what can I do?
I was playing in the garage one day,
And my face got blown off.

It didn't hurt as much as it does to look at you,

And know that that blast

Has kept me from you.

She doesn't respond to the poem when he leaves it for her. She ends up going out with this other guy, Jer, who is handsome.

The boy with the burned face gets another grenade. His dad had kept them, even after the accident. They were in a safe, but the boy knew the combination, *666*. He took the grenade and threw it into Jerry's car, when he was making out with the blond girl. The End.

After class, Shotts handed back the stories. At the bottom of mine he wrote, *What happened to the boy?* Then it said, *Talk to me after class. —Tom.* After class I went up to him. The other students were gone.

"What was that story about?" he said. He was still standing at the podium. He was such a gentle soul. He had longish gray hair and spectacles. He had had a heart attack, and he had almost died. He was frail.

I told him the story was about love.

"It's pretty violent," he said.

"Yup," I said.

"Was your dad in Vietnam?"

"No," I said. "My dad is Russian."

He asked if I lived with him, and I told him no, I lived with my stepdad, Harry. He asked about Harry. I told him that Harry had been in Vietnam.

"What happens to the boy with the burned face?"

"He lives happily ever after," I said.

"How could he? He killed two people? He would be caught and put in jail."

"Then he would kill himself."

That was a dumb thing to say. He was quiet after that. He looked at me, and his eyes looked watery, not like he was going to cry, but like he was very sensitive.

That night was the homecoming dance. I went, but I didn't go inside. I was with Ed and Teddy. We sat on the bleachers next to the baseball field and drank Kessler whiskey. Teddy used his fake ID, and we got more than a liter and a half for fourteen dollars. Across the blacktop we could see the people enter the gym. We were next to a sycamore, and its branches hung over us.

Ed was talking about an idea he'd had.

"What if your whole life is videotaped," he said. "It's on all these videotapes, and when you die you go to this little room and they're all sitting there and you have to watch the whole thing."

"They made a movie like that already," said Teddy.

"I know, but different from that," said Ed.

"If you watch your whole life, then it would be like, seventy more years, but just sitting there," I said. "It would be worse than life; you would have no control over what happens."

"No," said Ed. "Look, there is no *time* in heaven. It would be seventy years, or however long you live, but it wouldn't feel like that, it would just be a second. But you would have to face everything that you did."

"Why is it all on videotapes?" said Teddy.

"I don't know," said Ed. "That's not the point. I guess because I like the image of sitting there with all these tapes that say ED'S LIFE, and they're all labeled like some amateur did them."

"Maybe you could watch other people's tapes," I said.

"Yeah!" said Ed. "That would be great."

"Then if you talked shit about someone behind their back, they would know," said Teddy.

"That's right," said Ed. "So, it's pretty much like you have to just consider that they're watching it now. Like if you say something bad about Derek Cho, just act as if he were watching that video right when you said it."

"Derek *Cho*," said Teddy, and laughed.

"That guy's a fag," I said, and we all laughed.

Kessler whiskey always makes me sick. His picture was on the bottle, Julius Kessler. This old man, and above his head it said SMOOTH AS SILK. Later we all puked under the bleachers, and against the baseball fence.

After that, the guys wanted to go into the dance. I didn't want to go. They went in.

That night, Crissy Cort was sophomore homecoming princess. Jerry Holtz, her boyfriend, was sophomore homecoming prince.

I stayed under the tree for a while. Teddy and Ed ended up getting caught drunk. Teddy got suspended because he told the principal to fuck off. But I didn't know all that until later.

After a while of looking at the empty baseball field and waiting for something to happen, I walked home.

It took me a long time. I walked back up the train tracks. I opened my jacket and got the Altoids tin from the inside pocket, and I took out the second joint and the little red lighter. A night train passed. All the windows were lit up orange, like the inside of a large oven, rushing through the dark. I threw a rock at the back, and it bounced off.

I tried to balance on the track, but I kept falling off.

I saw Byron's green Porsche outside Guesthouse. I opened the knee-high gate in the white picket fence and followed the brick walkway around the house to the little guesthouse in back.

The door was unlocked, and I walked in. The lights were off except the light from the TV. Byron was slouched back on one of the black leather couches. There was no volume on the TV.

"Hi, Byron," I said. After a second he looked at me, and it was like he didn't recognize me. His eyelids were sitting heavy, halfway down his eyes. There was no emotion in his face.

I looked at the TV. MTV was on. It was Soul Asylum's "Runaway Train," but with no volume. I looked back to Byron. He wasn't looking at me anymore. He was just sitting there, in the almost dark, outlined by the changing rainbow of TV light. Like a hologram.

There was laughter from the back room. Mean mumbled laughter. I walked through Byron's line of vision to the back room. I opened the door slowly. There were a bunch of guys in there. They had music on the bedroom stereo, Bob Dylan. There was a girl on the bed, lying perpendicular, so her legs hung off the side. There were four guys standing with their backs to me. Jamie Berkof was in front of the girl. He was a big football player. His pants and underwear were down on top of his shoes. He had his hand on the wall over her head, to support himself. He did it really hard. I looked at her; her eyes were closed. It was Natasha Illichev. Her mouth moved without sentience. It wobbled open and closed with the motion. Sometimes her head would hit the wall, and the four guys would laugh softly.

I backed out of the door. I walked past Byron. On television, Kurt Cobain was swinging on a chandelier. Byron didn't say anything. I got out. It was cold outside. I didn't feel drunk anymore.

It felt like the blackness of the whole sky was opening up around me, like there was a lot of extra oxygen around me. I walked, and I was walking in a bubble.

I went home. Through the front window I saw Harry watching television in the front room. I walked around to the back door and went into my room.

I was crying. I thought about her rocking back and forth on the bed, about her face. I imagined her tongue inside her open mouth. I could see it in there. I took off my dad's jacket and grabbed a white shirt off my bed. I unbuttoned my pants and masturbated. I was thinking about her moist tongue in her mouth, like a little animal. Like a little heart, being rocked back and forth.

The next day was a Saturday. I slept late. Harry came in at noon and asked me to walk to the store to get some toilet paper. He put a ten-dollar bill on my desk. I was still in my clothes from the day before. I put on my dad's jacket and walked out.

I went past Guesthouse, but the green Porsche wasn't there. In Mollie Stone's there were some people, but not many. The crinkly faced woman was at the counter. I went to the toilet paper section and got a six-pack of Charmin Ultra Soft. It was only $5.99, so I went over to the chip section and got a bag of Fritos and a Coke.

I went to the counter and put the items on the conveyer belt. There was no one else in line. The old lady rang them up. When she was putting them in a bag she looked at me and said, "I know it was you."

"I'm sorry?" I said.

"Yesterday. I know it was you."

The guys dressed
as Coach Reese,
the on-campus security
guard

Acknowledgments

Thank you, Nicole Poor, my RISD friend. If I only got one thing
from art school, your friendship would be enough.
Thank you for the design of this book.

—

Thank you, Richard Abate, for believing in me and helping me
find an outlet for this kind of work.

—

Thanks to my family for the life experiences, for the love, and for
providing so much of this material.

—

The same goes for my old high school friends, especially
Ken Armistead, Tenaya Sims, Luke Paquin, Ivan Cross, Danny
Urman, J.R. Wilkinson, Matt Bunnell, Chris Young,
and my old girlfriend, Jasmine Seargeant.

—

Thanks to Palo Alto High School and all my teachers,
especially Woj.

—

Thanks to all my teachers at El Carmelo Elementary School
and all my teachers at J.L.S. and Jordan Middle Schools.

—

Thanks to the young friends and the Juvenile Bones Brigade.

—

Thanks to Ross and all the guys that helped me through.

—

Thanks to Josh Smith.

Read on for an excerpt from James Franco's
follow-up to *A California Childhood*

Hollywood Dreaming

Available from Insight Editions in September 2014

Bungalow 89

There I was in Bungalow 89, famous Bungalow 89, of the Chateau Marmont, the old hotel where the stars stay—tucked behind a wall, off Sunset Boulevard, just west of Laurel Canyon, right in the heart of Hollywood.

It was dusk.

Bungalow 89 is in the cottage area, apart from the main building, where the pool is, and the Ping-Pong table, where we had our mad tournaments in the past.

Bungalow 89 is not famous like Bungalow 3 (Belushi), or Bungalow 2 (*Rebel Without a Cause*). It is only famous in my own mind because it's where I first met Gus Van Sant, and because I eventually lived there for nine months. Back when I met Gus in this room, long ago, before I knew the Chateau or its ways, he sat in a comfy chair in the living room and played a little red lacquered guitar and talked to me; this was back when he was casting the supporting roles for his film about Kurt Cobain's last days alive, appropriately called *Last Days*—a slow-moving poetic rumination on what might have happened to Kurt before he blew off his head in the greenhouse. The role he liked me for eventually went to Lukas Haas, the kid from *Witness* with Harrison Ford, and one of the original Pussy Posse members, that unofficial social group centered around a younger Leo DiCaprio back in the '90s, post-*Titanic* and pre-Scorsese.

Lukas Haas had a gay sex scene in Gus's film. It was with Scott Green, the guy who talks about having to fuck a guy with a big cock in the *My Own Private Idaho* Chinese cafe scene—a testimony that was probably based on at least some reality—and who helped River

Phoenix do research for his young hustler role in the same seminal film. Which reminds me of a story Gus later told me about River in Portland, during preproduction, getting pulled over by the cops while he was wearing jeans with a hole so big in the front that his dick hung out.

But anyway, the gay sex scene in *Last Days*, the one with Lukas Haas and Scott Green, was ultimately cut out.

The Pussy Posse must have been alive around the time Leo shot *The Man in the Iron Mask* with the writer of *Braveheart,* and then *Celebrity*, with Woody Allen, where he plays an outrageous party-monster actor who trashes hotel rooms and flies around the world having fun with his celebrity—basically the paradigm for the show *Entourage.* A little trivia drop: Adrian Grenier, the eventual star of *Entourage*, essentially a show about the Leo character in *Celebrity,* was in *Celebrity*! As part of Leo's entourage! Go look: It's Adrian Grenier and, like, Sam Rockwell, or someone, being crazy with Leo—watch the way Leo shoves the champagne bottle between the young woman's knees in the limo. Or maybe I'm confusing the pretty boy from *Flags of Our Fathers* with Adrian, shit.

Around this time Leo was spotted by the crazy producer of *American Psycho* (who would eventually finance *Buffalo '66* and *Spring Breakers*) walking around the balcony of a high-rise in New York with a white parrot. Even though Christian Bale had been cast as Patrick Bateman, this crazy producer—let's call him *Crazy Producer*—made an offer to Leo for the role, which sent the movie's development into chaos. There was a moment when the casting was up in the air and Crazy Producer was at Cannes and he could claim that he had the star of *Titanic*, the most globally beloved film of teen females, *ever*, set to play the most despicable character in American literature in decades: a torturer and murderer of women. The concept was almost better than the actualization. And when I say *was almost*, I mean *was*.

This was the era—the high-flying New York period—when Leo was one of the cameramen on Harmony Korine's Andy Kaufman–inspired, drug-fueled experiment called *Fight Harm*, where Harmony picked fights with bouncers around the city and got beat up while his friends filmed it (David Blaine was also one of the cameramen). This project ended when a bouncer put Harmony's leg on the curb and jumped on it.

And, oh yeah, another memory: After doing *Milk*, Gus drove me around Portland, giving me the "*Idaho* tour." He showed me everything: the street in the heart of downtown where the real hustlers had stood, called *Camp* because it had been a squatters' camp back in the '30s and the name was passed on to the young hustlers of the '70s and '80s without them really knowing its origins; the condemned building that Keanu and River stayed in with the rest of the homeless kids, now a restaurant; and also a rundown motel where the production stayed during the first week of shooting, the week they shot the *This road looks like a fucked-up face* scene, and Keanu was ready to quit the film because he wasn't feeling good about his performance (it turned out to be one of his all-time best) and River came into Keanu's little hotel room, drunk from being in the bar with Udo Kier, and jumped on Keanu's bed and pretended to be the Incredible Hulk to make Keanu lighten up.

I sit in the comfy chair that Gus once sat in, strumming his little red guitar. Across the room is a painting of a boy dressed as a sailor with a red sailor cap. Except for his blondish hair (closer to my brother's color), he looks like me. A portrait of my ghost brother. I think that he is someone Gus would have liked.

Out my window, above the red ceramic tiles of the Spanish roofs, just to the left, is the billboard owned by Gucci, so close it is essentially part of the hotel, and on it is my oversized face, for you see I am a model for their fragrances, clothes, and eyewear. In this particular ad I am sitting in an old-fashioned blue Ferrari, with a goatee, looking out into the night—a concept designed by Nicholas Winding Refn, of *Drive* fame, of *Pusher* trilogy fame. His direction to me when we shot the Gucci commercial was always, "Less is more; *nothing is everything*." If I moved even an eyebrow, he'd come down on me with that little koan.

I think he used the same direction on *Only God Forgives.*

And I think of that billboard and what it's been for me, thanks to Gucci: that huge sign above Sunset, the main vein of Los Angeles. The time I clambered across the tiles and pulled myself up to the scaffolding beneath it—me, a small, scruffy speck in a Rolling Rock hat, and above me the Gucci version thirty times my size in a svelte black tux. And later, when Gus and I did the show at Gagosian, showing a new cut of *My Own Private Idaho* that focused mostly on River's character, Mike Waters (*Waters*, like *River*), calling it *My Own Private River*—Gucci let us use the billboard, and we put a photo of the back of River's head on it because the show (my recut of his film and his paintings of young men) was called *Unfinished*, and River lived a life that was unfinished.

This was the same weekend as the Oscars, the ones that I hosted, and behind the scenes of that show, that wonderful show, Terry Richardson shot photos; we had this plan to do a book together with photos (him) and poems (me) about the Oscars, and the Chateau and Lindsay Lohan, and we were going to come back to the hotel and do a shoot with Lindsay, who seemed to have been doing better at that point, but maybe wasn't actually. But I was so unhappy about the Oscar rehearsals because they had cut my Cher sequence—I was supposed to sing the song from *Burlesque,* "You Haven't Seen the Last of Me," dressed as Cher—that I didn't meet with Lindsay for the photos. Later she leaked a false story to the press that Terry was shooting a sex book involving her and me. Hilarious.

The book never happened, but I wrote a poem about her. It's in her voice, or a *version* of her voice—a kind of ventriloquism, a way to assume the "role" of Lindsay. Acting, playing the part of another actor, through poetry; mixed media. It's my version of a poem by Frank Bidart called "Herbert White," where Frank uses a psychopath as a mask to talk about some of his own feelings growing up gay in Bakersfield in the 1950s. Here is Lindsay, but really it is only a mask of Lindsay, like a Halloween mask. Just playing at being her, like Frank played at being a necrophiliac to talk about himself.

Herbert White *c'est* Frank. Lindsay Lohan *c'est moi.*

The Voice of Lindsay Lohan

Do you think I've created this?
This dragon girl, lion girl,
Hollywood hellion, terror of Sunset Boulevard,
Minor in the clubs, Chateau Demon?
Do you think this is me?

Lindsay Lohan,

Say it.
Say it, like you have ownership.
It's not *my* name anymore,
It's yours as much as mine.
So go ahead, say it.

Lindsay Lo-han.

Go ahead you bookworm punk
Blogger faggot, go ahead you
Thuggish paparazzi scumbag
With your tattoos and your
Unwashed ass—

You couldn't get a girl
If your life depended on it.
Does me in your blog
Make me yours?
Do your pictures capture me?

There is someone
Whom I have a strange
Relationship to
Who is called Lindsay,
Lindsay Lohan.

She's this strange actress
Who was very
Successful as a child;
People even said
She was talented.

And then she did a sweet
Teen thing called *Mean Girls*,
And then she did a lot of other things
That got her a lot of money
And a lot of fame.

And yes, she really was a mean girl.

But that fame raped me.
And I raped it, if you know what I'm saying.
How many young things selling movies, and wares,
And music and tabloids fucked the kind of men I fucked?
I was seventeen, eighteen, nineteen.

And everyone knew it,
But they let me in their clubs,
They let me have their drugs,
They stuck their dicks in me,
And now they stick their forks in me . . .

What do I fear?
Lindsay bitty Lohan.
And?
One night—the year
When all was right—

Before things got bad,
I was in New York
For the premiere of a film
I did with Robert Altman
And Meryl Streep;

After the movie I took James Franco
And Meryl's two young daughters to the club
Du jour, Bungalow 8
In the meatpacking district.
It was my place.

All my friends were there,
School friends, my mother
Looking her slutty best, bodyguards and Greeks.
We had our own table
In the corner, our own bottle.

I took two OxyContins
And things got bad.
The DJ was this bearded dude
Named Paul;
I remember requesting

Journey's streetlight people,
I remember sitting back down,
And I remember trying to speak up,
To talk to that cute boy
In a red gingham shirt, James.

My words rolled around
And got sticky
And didn't come out.
My friend from school
Kept talking to him,

Trying to be cute,
But she was only there because of me;
I told Barry, my bodyguard,
To take her away from our table.
And he banished her.

I took James back to the bathroom.
"You know why Amy put mirrors
All around in here?"
"Why?"
"So that you can watch yourself fuck."
He didn't fuck me, that shit.

And what was he doing there, anyway?
On *my* night. My night with Meryl,
My night when everything was right,
When I got everything I wanted.
Almost.

I fucked one of the Greeks instead,
A big-schnozzed, big-dicked,
Drunk motherfucker.
We did it in the bath.
That was the best night of my life.